THE
PEAK DISTRICT

by ROY CHRISTIAN

DAVID & CHARLES
NEWTON ABBOT   LONDON
NORTH POMFRET (VT)   VANCOUVER

BRITISH TOPOGRAPHICAL SERIES

Beyond the Great Glen
Bodmin Moor

In preparation

Pembrokeshire

ISBN 0 7153 7094 4
Library of Congress Catalog Card Number 75–26359

© ROY CHRISTIAN 1976

Set in 11 on 13pt Linotype Baskerville
and printed in Great Britain
by Latimer Trend & Company Ltd Plymouth
for David & Charles (Holdings) Limited
South Devon House   Newton Abbot   Devon

Published in the United States of America
by David & Charles Inc
North Pomfret   Vermont 05053   USA

Published in Canada
by Douglas David & Charles Limited
132 Philip Avenue   North Vancouver   BC

CONTENTS

ACKNOWLEDGEMENTS

MY thanks are due to many people who have helped in various ways in the writing of this book, so many that it would be impossible to mention them all by name. But I must mention the Editor of *Country Life*, for permission to use some material that has previously appeared in that magazine in a different form, and also Mr R. H. Appleby, for his valuable advice, Mr C. H. Sprenger, Mr Peter Legge, Mrs Frances Coe, for her astonishingly accurate and speedy typing, and, above all, Mr Frank Rodgers, who not only took all the photographs but also read the MS in draft and prevented many a slip through his tremendous knowledge of the Peak. I should be ungrateful if I did not also thank Mr J. W. Allen, who did so much to arouse my interest in the Peak and its history, and my wife and daughter who have not only been my companions in much of my wanderings around the area, but have also borne with fortitude my preoccupation with the writing of this book.

LIST OF ILLUSTRATIONS

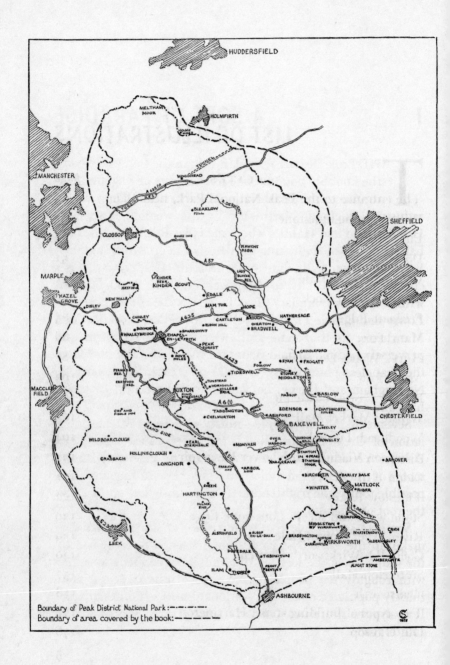

Boundary of Peak District National Park: —·—·—
Boundary of area covered by the book: — — —

1   A SORT OF PARADISE

THE Peak District is the last link in the Pennine Chain; the knobbly bottom bone in the spine of England. It is the coccyx freakishly cocooned within the heart of industrial England. Northward lie the woollen towns like Huddersfield and Halifax where men play Rugby League football, and massed choirs sing the *Messiah* in crowded, dignified Victorian town halls. Eastward, Sheffield Corporation buses climb out of the city to disappear into the Peakland mist within the city boundary. To the west is the country of L. S. Lowry and Gracie Fields: Oldham, Rochdale, Stockport and Manchester itself. To the south-west are those six towns that perversely became Arnold Bennett's 'five towns' and now form the shapeless pottery city of Stoke-on-Trent. Southward lie Nottingham and Derby; not far beyond, Leicester, Birmingham and Coventry.

Seventeen million people—nearly one third of the population of Great Britain—live within fifty miles of the Peak District. Yet one can find deeper solitude on the high gritstone moors of the Peak than almost anywhere else in England. It is possible to become frighteningly, dangerously lost up there on the roof of England.

Some 43,500 people live within the 542 square miles that make up the Peak District National Park. This is sparse by the standards of the surrounding industrial conurbations, but with roughly ten people to the square mile it is the most thickly populated of the ten National Parks so far designated. It is also the nearest to London—a mere three hours away by rail or road.

But the Peak Park does not include the whole of the Peak District. For various reasons, mainly because they were already marred by industrialism—especially limestone quarrying—some portions of the Peak were deliberately omitted from the Park. The most notable omission is a long, narrow enclave which bites deeply into the Park from New Mills in the west to encircle Buxton, and thus excludes from the Park what would have been its largest town and most obvious tourist centre. In the south-east Matlock, Cromford and Wirksworth are omitted, as is Ashbourne to the south. These places, along with Chapel-en-le-Frith and Glossop to the west, belong in spirit to the Peak and must be included in a book which deals with the whole area rather than simply with the National Park. For the same reason I shall extend the area south of Matlock to a line Ashbourne–Ambergate–Crich to include a stretch of country that I believe the Peak Park Joint Planning Board would like to enfold. This, then, as I see it, is the Peak District; a vaguely oval shaped wedge of land some forty miles long from north to south and about twenty-five miles across at its broadest, containing approximately 100,000 inhabitants.

The southern limit of the Peak District is also the southern limit of the highland zone of Britain and the boundary between northern and southern England, or between the North and the Midlands. Just where that boundary line comes is not easy to determine; it is as much a matter of atmosphere and personal impression as of exact geographical fact. Certainly it comes well north of the Trent, the traditional boundary between north and south. The BBC, in the days of regional broadcasting, drew their line between North and Midland regions through Brailsford and Belper, a few miles south of my line.

There is one spot of the A52 Derby–Ashbourne road where the boundary seems to be clearly definable. From Derby you drive north-westward over a midland landscape of rich, level grassland and gently rolling parkland. Then suddenly at a

8

bend in the road the land drops away into the valley of the Henmore, a tributary of the Dove. Below you, filling the valley, is Ashbourne, a small market-town of red brick and grey limestone; a frontier town where the New Red Sandstone of the Midland Plain meets the Carboniferous Limestone of the Peak District. Beyond, the green hills of the Peak, some grassy and rounded like the downs of the south, others sharply conical, march away to the misty horizon.

A mile farther west along the same road the Peakland boundary can be still more accurately placed. There the road crosses the Dove on the sinister sounding Hanging Bridge and abruptly starts a steep climb up Swinscoe Hill on the western flank of the Peak towards Leek, which is just outside the Park. The east side of the bridge manifestly belongs to lowland Britain and the west side equally obviously to the highlands. The Dove here is clearly the zonal boundary; it is also, for most of its 40 miles course to the Trent, the county boundary between Derbyshire and Staffordshire. And the odd thing here is that the Peak begins on the Staffordshire side, contrary to general belief, and it is the Derbyshire side that is flat.

This is one surprise confronting newcomers to the area; that the Peak District does not belong exclusively to Derbyshire. The Peak occupies about half of Derbyshire. Rather more than half the Peak Park lies in the county, and nearer the three-quarters of the Peak District covered in this book. But there are sizable chunks within the counties of Staffordshire and Cheshire and the Metropolitan counties of South Yorkshire (which includes Sheffield), West Yorkshire and Greater Manchester, though these are thinly populated, containing fewer than 7,000 inhabitants.

Another surprise to the uninitiated may be that there is no particularly high peak—no minor Matterhorn—to give the region its name. The highest part, Kinder Scout, is a boggy moorland plateau just over 2,000ft above sea level. The Peak is deceptively named. Its title derives not from some pointed summit but from a tribal group of early English settlers who occupied the territory thereabouts—the northern limit of the Saxon kingdom of Mercia—in the seventh century. They were called the Pecsaetans 'the hill dwellers'.

The Peak then must have been a desolate place, but as late as 1724 it was still 'a howling wilderness' in the words of Daniel Defoe that still rankle a little locally. Even by then, popular taste had not learnt to accept the beauty of wild scenery. True, there had been earlier eulogists of the Peak, but these were almost exclusively local propagandists imbued with patriotism and possibly even a vested interest in promoting the Peak. For instance, it was Thomas Hobbes, the philosopher, whose poem in Latin hexameters, *De Mirabilibus Pecci* (Concerning the Wonders of the Peak), appeared in 1636 and was subsequently reprinted several times, who spent more than half the ninety-one years of his life first as tutor and later as an honoured retainer in the Derbyshire homes of the Cavendish family who were then by far the largest owners of land in the Peak, and from the present sceptical age one is bound to question his motive in placing Chatsworth, the principal seat of his patrons, first among the 'Seven Wonders of the Peak', especially as the other six were all natural features. Charles Cotton, who exploited a similar vein to Hobbes in *The Wonders of the Peak* (1681), was another local man, living, when he was not enjoying London society or hiding from his creditors, at Beresford Hall in the heart of Dovedale.

Contemporary visiting writers tended to be cooler in their attitude to the Peak, some of them quite literally so. One remarked that he found it 'at least a topcoat colder' at the top of the hill out of Ashbourne on the Buxton road, and others were depressed by the Peakland climate, though generally the shivers that ran down the spines of these gentlemen—and one intrepid lady, Celia Fiennes, who toured the Peak on horseback in 1697—were induced as much by awe at the wildness of the scenery as by the temperature. Sir Thomas Browne's son Edward, a native of gentler East Anglia, expressed the general view of his contemporaries when he wrote of the Peak in 1662 as 'a strange, mountainous, misty, moorish, rocky, wild country', and there are days—and moods—even now when you feel that Browne had it exactly right.

But the Peak is neither always misty nor entirely wild. Its attraction rests partly in its grandeur, but even more in its variety and contrasts. It was the variety that impressed a more recent visitor, Sir John Betjeman, who wrote that in the northern half of Derbyshire—and his remarks could apply equally aptly to those sections of adjoining counties lying within the Peak—'stone never seems far below the surface, and stone of such variety, colour and quality as is found no-where else in Enlgand'.

So to understand the Peak you have to know about these stones. There are, as Sir John Betjeman implied, many varieties, but basically there are three main rock divisions: Carboniferous Limestone, Millstone Grit and shales.

Central Peakland, southward from the Hope Valley to the southern boundary, with inliers to the east at Crich and Ash-over—is a great dome of Carboniferous Limestone. This is the Low Peak, or White Peak because of the light grey limestone that outcrops impressively in such features as High Tor at Matlock and Cheer Tor, east of Buxton. Essentially it is a grassy plateau rarely rising much above 1,400ft or falling much below 900ft, with only a thin covering of soil above the limestone. It is an austere landscape of green fields divided into a chequer-board pattern by drystone walls, scattered, solid, limestone cottages—often built in a fold, with a thin belt of trees as an additional wind-break—and occasional villages in the same local stone, but it is saved from monotony because the rivers have cut deep, narrow, twisting and very beautiful trenches that are the famous Derbyshire dales.

'The whole glory of the country', it has been said, 'is in its

11

dales', and much of it certainly lies there. In such dales as Dovedale—generally acknowledged to be the finest of all— Monsal Dale, Chee Dale and Lathkill Dale the grass seems several shades greener and the slopes often so rich in vegetation—especially in ash trees—as to compensate for the bareness of the limestone uplands.

Not that all the dales are so luxuriant. Many of the higher ones are dry for most of the year. This is because limestone is slightly soluble in water. Rain-water, containing carbon dioxide which it has acquired on its way through the atmosphere, dissolves tiny particles of the rock on which it falls. The water then seeps down through the minute gaps it has created. Thus the limestone dome is a concealed cistern. Water lies only briefly on the upland surface, and in the dales some of the rivers tend to disappear in dry seasons. The Lathkill's upper reaches are usually dry; the Manifold, over the Staffordshire border, dives underground near Wetton Mill in dry weather to reappear 5 miles away in the grounds of Ilam Hall. The fissures down which the water runs are called swallow-holes, or swallets. The same denuding action of rain-water that causes them—and such caves as are not the result of lead mining—has carved strange shapes (sometimes beautiful, sometimes merely grotesque) in the rocks of Dovedale, in particular, that transcend the imagination of any human sculptor.

On three sides of the limestone belt runs a great horseshoe of darker rock. This is Millstone Grit, the raw material from which was shaped the Derbyshire millstones, piles of which still lie discarded on Stanage Edge and at the foot of Millstone Edge. The gritstone underlies the moors of the High (or Dark) Peak that provide some of the most savage, empty country in all England. Nothing much grows here but bilberries on the steep escarpments, heather on the slopes and cotton grass on the boggy tops of the plateaux. More than 10in of rain falls annually on these moors, the mean temperature in July is a mere 11° C, the sunshine rate is far below the national average, and mist is liable to close the visibility at almost any time. Yet it can be exhilarating country, offering on clear days wide views over open, untamed country and saved from utter desolation by the numerous streams that have carved themselves steep-sided valleys known locally as cloughs.

These gritstone moors taper off to a mere 2 miles in width in the extreme north of the Peak, but farther south, above the Vale of Edale, they widen out to 12 miles before dividing into the East and West Moors that flank the limestone belt to the southern limits of the area. The western escarpment of the East Moors runs in an almost unbroken series of razor-sharp 'Edges'—Stanage Edge, Millstone Edge, Froggatt Edge, Curbar Edge, Baslow Edge and Gardoms Edge—jagged with great boulders so that from the valley floor they resemble the scaly spine of some prehistoric monster.

The shales form a less easily definable area. Sometimes called the Edale Beds, or Yoredale Beds, they divide the limestone from the gritstone in the Edale and Hope valleys and overlie the limestone at the southern and south-eastern extremities of the area. They provide an easier passage for some of the rivers than do the harder rocks on either side. The Derwent, for instance, follows a shale outcrop for much of its course through a thickly wooded valley below the gritstone escarpment.

There are other rocks in addition to the three main types. Coal measures occur in isolated pockets, as in the Upper Goyt valley and near the headwaters of the Dane on the west and on Totley Moor and Ramsley Moor on the east. Basalt is fairly widespread. Locally it is called toadstone, either because of its dark and speckled appearance or from a corrupted form of what imported German lead miners called *todstein,* dead stone. Originally, toadstone was anything but dead, for it was molten lava that solidified to block the vents of now extinct volcanoes, like the two that overlook the Via Gellia near Grange Mill and another at Calton Hill, near Taddington. Dolerite is another igneous rock that appears at various places in the Peak.

Many of these rocks are worked commercially. As Celia Fiennes put it so eloquently, 'tho' the surface of these hills looks barren yet those hills are impregnated with rich Marbles Stones Metals Iron and Copper and Coale Mines in their bowels, from whence we may see the wisdom and benignitye of our greate Creator to make up the deffociency of a place by an equivolent as also the diversity of the Creation which encreaseth its Beauty'. Strangely, she did not specifically mention lead, which has been worked in the Derbyshire Peak for at least 1,900 years. Today the lead mining industry is virtually at an end, but its relics remain plentifully scattered over the limestone uplands.

Visible evidence of the former wealth and importance of the industry also remains. Some of the most lavish churches of Peakland, like Tideswell, the so-called 'cathedral of the Peak', Wirksworth and Youlgreave, are lead churches. They may be less numerous, less imposing than the great wool churches of the Cotswolds or East Anglia, but they are nevertheless impressive monuments to the prosperity of lead mining. Some of the profits from the mines and from rights in other minerals helped to build the splendid mansions at Haddon and Chatsworth. An even larger proportion went into the building of the numerous smaller Elizabethan or Jacobean manor houses that seem almost to grow out of the Peakland rock. Many of the smaller towns and larger villages—Wirksworth, Tideswell, Monyash, Youlgreave, Winster and Brassington, for instance—grew up as lead-mining centres.

Nowadays more wealth comes from the secondary minerals that the old-time lead miners threw away as rubbish. Thus it is the old spoil banks that are exploited for these gangue minerals such as fluorspar, barytes and calcite, though some mines have from time to time been reopened in the search.

Treak Cliff, near Castleton, still yields small quantities of a purplish-blue fluorspar called Blue John that was used for making ornaments that were highly fashionable in the eighteenth and nineteenth centuries.

There is a large Blue John vase at Chatsworth and others at Kedleston Hall, south of the Peak, surmounting Adam fireplaces that are themselves inlaid with Blue John. A local tradition that the Romans worked Blue John at Castleton lacks supporting evidence.

Few of the other minerals that Celia Fiennes noted are still worked today. The industrial archaeologist, for whom the area is a rich seam, will have to search diligently to find traces of the former coal pits or of the source of the Ashford marble —really a fine-grained limestone darkened by bituminous impurities—that is so effectively displayed in the chapel at Chatsworth, but his task will be considerably lightened if he arms himself with the excellent *Industrial Archaelogy of Derbyshire* by Frank Nixon and *Industrial Archaelogy of the Peak District* by Helen Harris. And he will find the substantial remains of the Ecton copper mines in the Manifold valley. Some of the profits from this enterprise were ploughed by the fourth Duke of Devonshire into the building of the splendid Crescent and its surroundings at Buxton in the eighteenth century.

The Peak District, then, has by no means escaped industrial exploitation, as the casual tourist imagines. Where it was fortunate was in getting much of its industrial revolution out of its system early, leaving behind mostly only relics that have acquired the interesting patina that comes with age. The industrial revolution in the cotton industry virtually began at Cromford, in the south-east of the area, where Sir Richard Arkwright built the first water-powered cotton mill and laid the foundation of his great cotton empire. His surviving mills around there, some of them still involved in the textile industry, only add to the attractions of that part of the

Derwent valley. Some of Arkwright's money financed the building of Samuel Oldknow's mill at Mellor on the north-western edge of the Peak, not far from Glossop and New Mills that developed slightly later as far outposts of the Lancashire-based cotton industry. These places are no longer exclusively textile centres, but they are unmistakably industrial towns and make no claims to beauty—though Glossop has more than immediately meets the eye. However, they do cling to the valleys where the streams race down from the gritstone moors; so they can be taken or left alone. They do not intrude into the Peak itself, so they do not jar like the great cement works that sticks up its smoking chimney out of the Hope Valley at Bradwell, or like the monstrous limestone quarries.

Derbyshire has more limestone quarries than any other county in Britain except Yorkshire, if one accepts Yorkshire as a single county. Almost all are in the Peak District, along with several Staffordshire quarries. In fact quarrying—including some less obtrusive gritstone quarries—is the main source of employment in the Peak; it is also the main source of pollution. Limestone dust clings to the trees in Middleton Dale, discolours the river Wye at the foot of Topley Pike and conspicuously mars the landscape in a score of places. Quarrying has a long history in the Peak, and disused quarries, especially when partly hidden by interesting flora, often fit agreeably into the landscape; indeed the scarred but shining face of Crich Quarry is a much revered feature that to many people marks the southern end of both the Peak District and the Pennine Chain. But modern limestone quarrying has become big business and its products are in enormous demand not only for industry but also in the making of roads. Satisfying these demands—and reaping the accompanying profits—involve large-scale workings, vast machines and a good deal of mess.

To be fair, the pollution is probably no worse than it was two centuries ago when travellers complained bitterly of the

sulphur smells and thick smoke that hung over Stoney Middleton and along the road between Buxton and Ashbourne. But
the point is that we have stopped learning to live with it, and
rightly so. And though intensive quarrying has arrested the
decay of many old lead mining villages by turning them into
quarry villages, it is also slicing some 2sq miles of limestone
100ft high out of the Peak Park every year and doing even
more damage beyond the fringes of the Park.

How to reconcile the national and local economic needs
with the equally pressing need to conserve and protect some
of our most beautiful countryside is a problem that concerns
all the local authorities that administer parts of the Peak District and weighs particularly heavily on the Peak Park Joint
Planning Board, which has the statutory duty 'to conserve and
enhance the natural beauty of the area'. It is a problem that
is likely to become more acute in the future. So far, the Board,
the first to be set up under the National Parks Act of 1949, has
prevented major extensions to quarries within the Park, and
has had co-operation from some quarry owners in tidying up
derelict sites. But there have been major extensions to quarries
just outside the Park boundaries, particularly at Tunstead,
the largest limestone quarry in Europe. Any further developments here would threaten the Park.

The Board faces other problems. One concerns water. The
Dark Peak is a huge catchment area for water. Already there
are 51 reservoirs within the Park, including 3 that have been
constructed since the Board began its life in 1951, and 22
more just outside. Some of these, like the Ladybower and
Derwent Reservoirs—the latter used for training by RAF
'Dam Buster' crews in World War II—are popular with those
tourists who are unconcerned about a degree of urbanisation
in hitherto wild country. Others, like the new Errwood
Reservoir in the Goyt Valley, fit happily into the second of
the Board's main duties—'to provide and promote facilities
for the enjoyment of the National Park'—by providing oppor-

tunities for sailing. But where will it stop? We as a nation were consuming 14 million cubic metres of water a day—over 3,000 million gallons—in 1972. Planners except double that to be going down the national drain by the end of the century. So unless somebody comes along with a less land-consuming scheme—like desalination or tidal barrages—it looks as if more land will disappear under the water, with an attractive valley at Carsington, just south of the Park, as possibly the next sacrificial candidate.

The motor car is another problem. Every year 16 million people visit the Peak, and most of them travel there by car, mainly between Easter and September. This puts extra pressure on roads already carrying much heavy goods traffic, especially lorries loaded with stone from the quarries. But the Peak Park Joint Planning Board has firm ideas about traffic control. Having banned traffic from some narrow roads in the Goyt Valley on Sundays in high summer—and provided a mini-bus service to carry people around that area—it is now channelling lorry traffic on to certain roads in the Peak, leaving others, more scenically attractive, free for pleasure motoring and reducing disturbance to local communities.

Much potential through traffic has already been diverted from the Peak on to the M1, running just east of the area, and the M6 to the west. The M62 carries traffic across the Pennines just to the north, and when the M42 is built to cross south Derbyshire the Peak will be closed within a motorway box that will make access convenient from all sides without damage to the scenery. Unfortunately this happy arrangement is threatened by a proposed Sheffield–Manchester motorway that would cut through the Peak Park only 12 miles south of the M62. Such a road would be a needless intrusion on a wild landscape, as the Board has forcibly pointed out, but, ironically, it is more likely to be the economists rather than the environmentalists who may stop this particular piece of nonsense.

I am not suggesting that the Peak is no place for the motorist. The roads are generally good, and if such bottle-necks as Matlock, Bakewell and Ashbourne are avoided on fine Sunday evenings, motoring in the Peak can be pleasurable. In the Low Peak, especially, there are numerous good minor roads running through attractive scenery and almost devoid of traffic, though a drive across the grain of the country from Chesterfield in the east to Leek in the west may bring doubts about the aptness of the 'Low' adjective. Most of the main roads thereabouts run north and south along river valleys. The A6, using the valleys of the Derwent and Wye, is a scenically splendid road that virtually bisects Derbyshire, and the road that leaves it at Rowsley to follow the Derwent through Chatsworth Park and then climbs over the moors from Baslow to Owler Bar and on to Sheffield offers a superb variety of scenery. Further north, where the main roads run east and west, the A57 over the Snake Pass is one of the most wildly dramatic main roads in England as well as one of those most often closed in winter by bad weather.

But much of the best Peakland scenery is hidden from the motorist. This is equally true of the gritstone moors in the north and the limestone dales farther south. The Peak District is a walker's paradise, offering something for every kind of walker. The hardy-boots-and-haversack brigade can find really tough going in the Kinder Scout and Bleaklow area, including the first thirty miles or so of the Pennine Way (officially opened in 1965) as it winds northward from Edale to Kirk Yetholm on the Scottish border 250 miles away. But this sort of 'bog trotting' should only be attempted by those who are properly equipped in every sense. A peat bog in mist and sleet is no place for the afternoon stroller in city shoes and without a compass, as the Peak District Mountain Rescue teams know only too well. Less ambitious ramblers can find pleasure and security on the Tissington Trail, which follows the trace of the former Ashbourne–Buxton railway line, or the High Peak

19

Trail, which joins it on the limestone uplands having climbed up from the Derwent Valley along the track of the famous Cromford & High Peak Railway. Between these extremes are the Dales, where the views may be more limited in distance but unlimited in beauty. Walkers have the whole of Dovedale to themselves, and the finest parts of the Manifold, Hamps, Wye and Lathkill.

For those who want something more adventurous than either motoring or walking—which can, as I say, be hazardous enough for the unwary—there is gliding from Great Hucklow and a ski-run at Edale. Cavers and pot-holers find plenty of opportunity to test their courage and skill in the Peak, and the rock climber is richly rewarded on the gritstone edges, where several Everest men have served their apprenticeships.

Quieter tastes are equally well satisfied. The little towns are gracious, welcoming, and blend well with their surroundings. Buxton, the second highest market town in England at 1,000ft above sea level, has the best range of accommodation, shops and entertainment, thermal springs with a constant temperature of nearly 82° F, but a rainfall of more than 48in a year. Matlock is a slightly smaller, more boisterous resort, locally celebrated for its autumn illuminations, and undeniably beautiful, though the sensitive visitor may be slightly discouraged by a slight aroma of fish and chips at weekends. Bakewell, where the Peak Park Joint Planning Board has its offices and an excellent information centre in the seventeenth-century maket hall, is a charming little town ringed by green hills in the lush valley of the Wye. It is an ideal centre for those who want a quieter, drier and less hilly alternative to Buxton. Ashbourne, almost equally charming, is the traditional 'gateway to Dovedale' and has architecturally the best street in Derbyshire. Wirksworth is smaller, more rugged and totally unselfconscious; an old lead-mining centre turned quarry town, with attractive little byways leading to its ancient church.

The villages may lack the gaiety of their honey-coloured counterparts in the Cotswolds or the strangely underestimated Rutland, but there is not an ugly one amongst the lot, though the upland settlements could be too austere for some tastes. The more typical village, however, sits on a shelf some eight hundred feet up with its back to a higher hill that acts as a wind-break. Almost all are built of limestone or gritstone, or a combination of the two at places like Hartington where both kinds of rock are close at hand, and most older houses have roofs of the local 'slate' which is, in fact, gritstone.

Two villages demand special attention for reasons other than their outward attractions: Eyam because of the heroism of its people who chose to live—and die—with the plague of 1665 rather than to leave and risk spreading the germs elsewhere; Tissington for its famous well-dressing custom. Other Peakland villages now dress their wells and springs, but this folk-art, now almost exclusively confined to Derbyshire, almost certainly originated at Tissington.

The Peak is particularly rich in customs and folk legends. This is largely because of its relative isolation before the arrival of the motor car and of the reluctance of its people to accept change. Peakrills are hardy, hardworking, taciturn people, not given to displays of emotion or to revealing their warmth of heart. They are doers rather than thinkers, traditionalists rather than innovators, a generalisation immediately confounded by the thought that the Peak's most notable native was probably that great innovator James Brindley, father of the canal system; which shows the dangers of generalising about people in general and Peak people in particular.

The comparative isolation that has kept the Peak out of the main stream of national history has also acted against dramatic population changes. Many villages on the western side of the Peak have fewer inhabitants now than they had in the mid-nineteenth century when lead mining still flourished.

Only on the east has there been modest expansion, mainly in the last thirty years or so when some villages have tended to become outer dormitories of Sheffield, less than thirty minutes' drive away. There is a danger that the places may become single-class villages of wealthy commuters, with the indigenous villagers being driven by the rising price of cottages to live in council estates on the fringes like Red Indians on their reserves. Though this has not yet become the reality that it is in parts of Cheshire and the Home Counties, the writing has already appeared on the walls of such delectable places as Ashford-in-the-Water, Curbar, Hathersage and Padley.

Happily there is no such writing on those grey drystone walls that stride across the uplands. Up there things have changed litle outwardly for two centuries or more; nor have they on the heather-clad gritstone moors or down in the cloughs and dales. That there have been changes will emerge, I hope, in the subsequent chapters, but they have been gradual—evolutionary rather than revolutionary—and not all for the worse by any means.

One change for the better that must be mentioned here is that for most days in the year it is possible to walk quite freely on the moors of the Dark Peak. A century ago that was almost out of the question. Even seventy years ago J. B. Firth wrote of the 'extraordinarily few footpaths' on which the public were permitted to walk, 'and if you deviate you do so at your peril'. And the peril he meant was not from the weather but from gamekeepers. 'The High Peak . . . is sacred to grouse.' So it remained, despite the efforts of men like C. H. B. Ward, founder of the Clarion Ramblers Club, Tom Stephenson, and thousands of others who fought—sometimes literally—to gain public access to the moorland. The mass trespass of ramblers and walkers on Kinder Scout in 1932 is now part of the folk history of the Peak. But the National Parks Act of 1949 and the efforts of the Peak Park Joint Planning Board have made further demonstrations unnecessary. Today, though the land is still privately owned, the public have access to 76sq miles of open country and gritstone edges except on a few days each year during the grouse shooting season between 12 August and 10 December.

In addition, they have access to the dales and many miles of footpaths and bridleways through richly varied country that has the appearance of having remained unchanged over the centuries. It is because the Peak is so apparently little altered; because it still offers the simple things that many of us want—spacious country interspersed with intimate green dales, a leisurely way of life or the chance of adventure—that it is one of the most deeply loved parts of Britain. When Dr Richard Russell wrote in the eighteenth century of 'a sort of Paradise' he was thinking specifically of Matlock, but for many people it could still be used to sum up the whole of Peakland.

2 THE MAKING OF THE LANDSCAPE

THE landscape of Britain is a blending of nature and nurture. There are parts of the country—especially the south-east—where nurture predominates and you have to look carefully and imaginatively to see the natural landscape. In the Peak District the position is reversed. More than in most other parts of England you see the natural landscape, though even here man has tinkered away at it, adding here, taking away there. But his efforts over the last few thousand years amount to little more than a touching up of the picture that nature took some 280 million years to paint.

Such a time-scale is difficult to comprehend. I remember some twenty years or so ago telling a bored, sceptical class of boys that 280 million years before the whole area of what is now Peakland was covered by a shallow sea that was sometimes clear and sometimes muddy, under which was gradually built up from the shells and bodies of minute organisms and from decaying stone-lilies a pile of detritus nearly 2,000ft thick. To this they sensibly objected that either the tip of this mass must have appeared above the surface or I must have misled them about the shallowness of the sea. My reply that the foundations of these deposits were subsiding gently all the time was regarded as an inspired evasion, and the information that all this debris eventually consolidated into the calcitic rock known as Carboniferous Limestone left them as cold as the rock itself.

But a few days later when I took these same boys up on to the limestone uplands near Castleton, one of them came running to me with a perfect fossil sea-snail in his hand. 'It was right what you said, sir,' he gasped, 'about all this being under the sea. It didn't mean nothing to me then, sir, but it does now.' And I felt obliged to admit that only at that moment was it beginning to mean much to me either. You really need some evidence of that sort to bring this almost incredible story to life.

The Castleton area is rich in this sort of fossil evidence. More than seventy different species of brachiopod, or lamp-shell, have been identified in Treak Cliff alone. Brachiopods are bivalve shellfish. It was accumulations of fossil brachiopods, along with corals and molluscs, that built up reefs, and it is possible by plotting the distribution of these fossils to see that in earliest times an irregular chain of reefs surrounded a lagoon some 20 miles long and 10 miles wide whose bed was composed mainly of crinoid—sea-lilies—coral and shell-sand. The lagoon is now the central limestone area of the Peak. The reefs that fringed it are the richest areas for fossil hunters in the Peak: the hills of the mid-Dove, Lathkill Dale, parts of Bradwell and Middleton Dale, and High Tor.

Outside the reefs lay deeper water into which was washed mud from the rivers farther north to become the Edale Shales. Later, coarser sediments—grit and gravel—were carried down from the same direction to form sandbanks that eventually became what we know today as the Millstone Grit series. And while this gradual process continued, occasional small submarine volcanoes erupted to throw out their lava which solidified to become the local 'toadstone',

Sometimes the land rose above the water. Water-borne seeds and wind-driven spores settled and germinated in the warm, moist climate to form a tropical forest in which primitive four-legged newt-like creatures moved and had their being. Gradually the debris from the trees and plants became peat. When the land sank again below the waters the peat became buried under mud and clay and, as a result of this pressure and the chemical reaction that followed, changed into coal, while the mud above it became shale.

This rising and sinking of the land was repeated several times, its results being recorded in the layers of grits and shales visible today. Above the black shales of the first inundation comes the thin, shaly sandstone that gives the 'shivers' to the face of Mam Tor. The Shale (or Pendle) Grit above is firmer without being entirely stable. The content of the next sandwich, between two layers of shale, is altogether tougher. This is the Kinder Grit that forms the top of the Kinder–Bleaklow plateaux. The Chatsworth (or Rivelin) Grit —again sandwiched between layers of shale—is equally firm. The next grit layer—Haslingden Flag—is a parsimonious filler indeed in the Peak, though it is more thickly spread farther north in Lancashire. Uppermost is a coarser, crumbling layer sometimes called the First Grit.

Subterranean pressures then worked for millions of years to crumple the Carboniferous rocks into a series of folds, giving the effect of a table-cloth that has been roughly pushed in from the sides. The broadest fold, running north and south —'like an irregular and elongated dome', in the words of Patrick Monkhouse—is what geologists now call the Derbyshire Dome, and is basically what most of us call the Peak District. The eastern side of this dome rises fairly gently; the west more sharply. In places there are faults, or rock-fractures. The A625 road follows the line of one fault as it passes between Mam Tor and Treak Cliff, and the road between Foolow and Eyam runs along the line of another.

When the crests of the folds were thrust upwards they were immediately attacked by frost and rain, which scraped off the accumulation of clays, shales, fine sandstone and coal seams— known collectively as the Coal Measures—to deposit their debris in the lowlands, leaving the Millstone Grits exposed to the same abrasive forces. The grits, however, were harder, and only in the south of the area were they worn away so completely as to expose the limestone core. The Derbyshire Dome came to resemble the head of an ageing man, bald on the crown but with tufts of hair on three sides.

The erosion and the slight sinking of the land went on after the folding ceased. Debris from distant mountains added to the existing piles in the lowlands until the whole of the Peak District was buried under waste. This burial lasted for the whole of the Mesozoic Era, about 120 million years, during the later part of which the whole of Britain except the Scottish and Welsh mountains was covered by a clear warm sea. Then Britain rose, as we used to sing at school with more enthusiasm than conviction, 'out of the azure main', but very gradually, not, as I used to imagine, like a dolphin leaping out of the water.

The streams of water that poured off the central dome during this gradual rise helped to wear away the younger rocks and expose again, even to cut into, the Carboniferous rocks, following the courses they had cut through the younger rocks and ignoring the folds of the older rocks below. It is this superimposed drainage system that accounts for the wide variety of scenery that is found along the Peakland rivers. But the scenery of the Peak—or of any piece of land—is entirely superimposed, to use the word in a less technical sense. It is, if you like, the detail that has been painted into the outline that was drawn of the Peak District some 15 million years ago.

It is the detail that is the attraction of the Peak, and it owes only a little to that period of alternating warm spells and polar conditions that is popularly known as the Great Ice Age. Although ice from the Irish Sea penetrated the valley of the Derwent as far south as Matlock, its chief effect on the scenery can be seen in the north-west, where there are moraines in the Goyt Valley at Taxal and in the Todd Valley near Whaley Bridge. The glacial lakes that once covered the Chapel-en-le-Frith area were drained by overflow channels that can still be seen near Lyme Hall and Disley. Here and there you may find an odd boulder that has been pushed down from the north by ice, or an occasional valley that may have been scored by a glacier, but none of these things amount to much.

The rivers and streams, as I have already suggested, have had far more influence in shaping the face of the Peak. Most of the main rivers rise on the gritstone. They then take the most convenient route off it, which often leads them in very different directions. Take the Derwent, for instance, the Peak's longest river. It rises on the east side of the Bleaklow ridge and, after some early hesitations, settles down to flow south-eastward to join the Trent some sixty miles distant, having collected on its way, among other tributaries, the Noe, from the peat bogs above Edale, the Wye, from Axe Edge, and the Amber, which comes down from the gritstone above Ashover. But the Etherow, rising a few miles north of the Derwent, settles immediately for a western course. A few miles east of Stockport it joins the Goyt, which has come down from Axe Edge and disputes with it the claim to be the true source of the Mersey. The Dane, which rises only two miles from the Goyt, also ultimately flows into the Mersey after following a more southerly course that takes it down into the Cheshire Plain. Yet the Dove, and its tributary the Manifold, rise close together only a few miles south of the Goyt and Dane, and follow companionable courses in a south-easterly direction before they join forces and eventually flow into the Trent, which has itself come down from the western side of the Pennine watershed not far outside the Peak.

But the point to make here is that all these rivers begin life as mountain streams, rushing down from the gritstone, pushing before them any rocks or boulders that stand in their way and using them as a stone mason uses a chisel to scrape away at the rocks below and on either side. Fifteen million years or so of that sort of treatment is more than even the hardest rocks can withstand. By this vertical erosion the Peak-land rivers have scoured out deep trenches. And on either

28

side of them, rain and frost have helped to weather away the valley sides to form the superb Dale scenery.

To follow the Dove from its source is perhaps the best introduction to Peak scenery. Its source on Axe Edge is just east of the A53 Buxton–Leek road, opposite Dove Head Cottage. A stone above the source spring bears the intwined monograms of Izaak Walton and Charles Cotton, though it is likely that the lettering was the work of some nineteenth-century romantic.

Above the village of Hollinsclough the stream is unremarkable, except that it runs a little above the bottom of its own valley instead of taking the easier way, thus making its own point about superimposed drainage. Between Hollinsclough and Earl Sterndale two extraordinary conical hills, Chrome and Parkhouse, dominate the left bank. Both are narrow, with steep sides rising to sharp serrated edges like spear points. These are reef knolls, examples of the kind of coral reefs, mentioned earlier, that were formed by myriads of polyps in the Carboniferous sea and were thus less easily dissolved than the surrounding limestone. These hills and their surroundings are rich in marine fossils.

High Wheeldon (1,348ft) the next hill of note is more conventional in shape, and indeed the next five miles or so through Crowdecote and on to Hartington are fairly orthodox geologically. The river runs through a layer of black shales. On the east side of the widened valley runs an even ridge of grass-covered limestone. On the west the facing ridge is set out like a textbook, with the whole gamut of sandstones, shale grit and shales, with a fragment of Kinder Grit to cap Sheen Hill (1,247ft). 'Here', wrote Patrick Monkhouse, 'is perfect geological conformity, and like all conformity it is respectably dull.'

But conventionality ends at Beresford Dale, where the Dove breaks through into the limestone. From then on, through Wolfscote Dale, Mill Dale and into Dovedale proper is sheer delight for both geologist and layman. Dovedale itself is a narrow ravine carved out by river action, its massive sides fissured and weathered into fantastic shapes, the dramatic effect heightened by the numerous loops in the river that show you a series of sharp close-up pictures of succeeding short stretches, each more breathtaking than the previous one.

The best examples of frost weathering are the fan-shaped screes of limestone fragments—superbly described locally as 'slitherbanks'—near Iron Tors in Wolfscote Dale and at various other places. The Dove Holes, close to where Hall Dale runs off the main dale, are two great arched recesses in the rock, the larger having a span of 55ft and a height of 30ft, but neither runs more than a few feet back into the hillside. They were formed by tributary streams that were drained when the Dove deepened its own channel below their level.

Reynard's Cave, a little farther downstream, was formed in the same way. The great feature of Reynard's is its detached doorway, a natural arch of limestone 40ft high and 18ft wide. But be careful of Reynard's Cave. It lies temptingly close above the footpath on the left bank of the river—but the rough track up to it is steep and slippery whatever the weather. An Irish dean once tried to ride up it on horseback with a girl riding pillion, like a modern young man showing off on a motorbike. The horse slipped, all fell and rolled down the slope. The dean died from his injuries and was buried in Ashbourne churchyard.

Dovedale is no place for showing off, though nature does it superbly. Without human aid it has carved Lion Rock into a most creditable representation of that most noble beast. By denudation it has carved spires and pinnacles in rock. Pickering Tor, Ilam Rock, Tissington Spires and the Twelve Apostles are all gigantic monoliths, remnants of spurs that once projected into the gorge. Frost has attacked from both sides of the spurs, working its way along the main joints to cut them away from the spurs. Rain-water containing dissolved carbon dioxide then took over to dissolve the corners and edges and produce the splendid pinnacles you see today.

Facing the Twelve Apostles, the riverside footpath climbs over Lover's Leap, a spur which has withstood large-scale denudation. Round the next bend two more reef knolls, Thorpe Cloud and Bunster, close the end of the dale above the much-photographed stepping stones where the crowds gather at weekends. Half a million visitors a year tramp the footpath on the Derbyshire side of the Dove and create a new example of denudation. The top surface of the path has been worn away to an extent that further regeneration of the vegetation is impossible and remedial work has had to be carried out to give the path a firmer surface that will stand up to the pressure of 'boots marching up and down again'.

But enough, for the moment, of the Dove, though one can never really have enough of this prince of rivers. There are, though, other rivers that are geologically interesting as well as scenically beautiful. The Manifold reproduces some of the features of the Dove. At Apes Tor, near Hulme End where the river trenches the limestone, you can see that limestone grotesquely tilted and contorted. There are splendid caves formed in the same way as those on the Dove, though some, like Thor's Cave, are much higher above the present course of the river. And there are the swallets, as indeed there are in its tributary the Hamps. The Peakland rivers deserve a later chapter to themselves, but there is one other that must be mentioned now for its geological interest.

This is the Lathkill, one of the few rivers that rise on the limestone. Its exact source fluctuates with the weather. In an averagely wet winter it rises impressively in Lathkill Head (or House) Cave in Ricklow Dale, just below Monyash, rather as the cascade at Chatsworth emerges from its grotto on the hill above the mansion. In drier weather the river rises almost furtively among the rocks from a number of small springs some half a mile lower down the valley. After the long dry spring of 1974 it emerged lower down still, beyond Over Haddon, and 500 fish had to be carried to safety further downstream. Its real source is underground. The rain-water has seeped through cracks and joints and the growing river has carved its own subterranean channel from which it emerges sooner or later depending on how full this channel is down below.

So the limestone country has its own exciting watery underworld. There are miles of natural underground tunnels, some of which were found—occasionally with disastrous results—by lead miners. Indeed cavers have traced the Lathkill water back to underground lead mine workings between Monyash and Flagg. But it is the natural passageways and caves we are concerned with now. All were formed by the action of water for ever dissolving the limestone around it until it found its natural water table when there were no more cracks and fissures to fill.

Some underground streams emerge dramatically from cave mouths, like the Lathkill. The Wye runs underground for some distance in Poole's Cavern at Buxton, and Peakshole Water, a tributary of the Noe, emerges from the still more spectacular entrance of the Peak Cavern at Castleton. Known until the squeamish nineteenth century by a more graphic but less generally acceptable name, Peak Cavern was described as a 'marvel of England' as early as the twelfth century and subsequently appeared on almost everyone's list of 'wonders of the Peak', though Daniel Defoe, cynically indifferent to natural wonders, dismissed it with something approaching contempt.

Most of the numerous Derbyshire caves occur, as Professor K. C. Edwards has pointed out, on the margins of the limestone where streams come down from the gritstone and where the limestone is frequently of the highly soluble reef type.

Page 33 (above) Entrance to the Peak National Park, near Ilam. Thorpe Cloud is the conical hill on the right; *(below)* winter on the limestone

Page 34 Eldon Hole, one of the traditional 'wonders of the Peak'

The dissolving action of the water has carved as many strange shapes in the rock below ground as above. Celia Fiennes found one in Poole's Cavern 'lookes like a Lyon with a Crown on his head', and another 'lookes just like the shape of a large Organ with the severall keys and pipes one above another as you see in a great Cathedrall', and in many caves there are most impressive displays of stalactites and stalagmites—caused by calcite deposits—that have delighted visitors and enriched the tourist trade for nearly three centuries.

Potholes are less common in the Peak than in the Yorkshire Dales and only two of these large swallow holes can be seen on the surface of the landscape. These are Eldon Hole and Nettle Pot, on opposite sides of Eldon Hill. Eldon Hole is the better known because it was another of the 'wonders of the Peak' and was popularly believed by the ancients to be bottomless. However, there is a bottom at little more than 180ft where, potholing friends tell me, there are piles of boulders and an abominable smell from the rotting carcases of dead sheep that have fallen down the 20ft wide shaft.

Another 'wonder of the Peak' was the ebbing and flowing well. There are, or were, two of these: one above Barmoor Clough, near Chapel-en-le-Frith, the other in a cottage garden at Tideswell. Celia Fiennes and some of her contemporaries had vague ideas that these springs that gushed out intermittently were caused by the action of the tides and that Tideswell derived its name from this phenomenon. But the appearance of the springs was due to excessive water in the underground channel, and Tideswell was simply the spring or well belonging to Tid, who is presumably buried on Tideslow nearby. The well at Tideswell ceased to function when a new drainage system was laid out in the village early in this century, but the Barmoor Clough one is said to perform occasionally after heavy rain, though I have never managed to see it in action myself.

The so-called petrifying wells of Matlock Bath impressed

C

me much more when I was a boy because it seemed that objects such as birds' nests and bowler hats held in the well turned to stone. What actually happened was that the objects were covered with a hard coating of lime set free by rapidly diminishing pressure from springs rising from a considerable depth. Water flowing from springs of this sort of depth over wet surfaces causes moss to grow and to extract carbon dioxide from the water so that it no longer holds much lime in solution. This lime covers the moss to form a spongy rock called tufa. A cottage in the Via Gellia is built entirely of this material. It is called, unsurprisingly, Tufa Cottage.

If I dwelt at length on the shaping of the limestone scenery this is not because the landscape of the grits and shales lacks interest; far from it. 'Malicious country', a lady in Holmfirth said, nodding her head sharply in the direction of the gritstone 'tops'. She proceeded to tell me of a neighbour of hers who went up on to the 'tops' one winter evening to carry out a routine inspection at one of the reservoirs and did not come back alive. His body was found a week or so later. He had died of exposure, lost in a landscape he had known all his life. But if the country bears malice towards some, it is for others the most exciting and rewarding part of the Peak District.

Up on the gritstone is the Peak's only substantial waterfall, Kinder Downfall. In a dry summer it can be a disappointing sight; a mere trickle of water seeping from a shelf of rock. But such dry spells are comparatively rare on Kinder, which averages 63in of rain a year at its northern edge and more than 60in in the neighbourhood of the Downfall, which is perhaps seen at its best when the mad March winds—and winds up there can be March-mad in any month—are blowing the spray around so ferociously that you get the illusion that the waterfall is flowing uphill; or on winter days when the water freezes so that the Downfall becomes a spectacular series of icicles.

The stream that feeds the Downfall is one of many that rise on the gritstone and have carved deep, narrow channels through successive layers of grits on their way towards such rivers as the Derwent or the Etherow in the north or the Dane and the Goyt in the west. Little channels eating their way through peat are known locally as 'groughs', but they are seldom important enough to justify a name on the maps. But two or three of these streams joining forces push their way through the grits to form narrow but impressive cloughs with romantic-sounding names like Ravens Clough, Wildboar Clough, Oaken Clough and Dovestone Clough. Such cloughs are most numerous on the western side of the gritstone country, especially round the upper reaches of the Goyt and Dane, but one of the most attractive and extensive lies farther east. This is Bretton Clough, a deep cutting between Abney Low (1,338ft) and Sir William Hill (1,407ft), which is less well known than it deserves to be, partly because of its distance from the nearest main roads and partly because no footpath runs along its whole length, though several cross it.

The Millstone Grit has, of course, been subject to the same processes of erosion as the limestone. Sometimes the younger grits have been worn away to leave such splendid hill forms as Grindslow Knoll (1,805ft) on either side of the river Noe at the eastern end of the vale, and Shutlingsloe (1,659ft), a conical hill with a sharp tilt of rocks at the eastern side of the summit. Win Hill and Lose Hill are examples of cliffs that have collapsed as a result of water seeping from the gritstone plateaux to soften and squeeze out the adjoining shale until the foundations have been undermined. Large plateaux, like Stanton Moor, west of the Derwent Valley, have been much reduced in size by the same process.

Close to Stanton Moor are large outcrops of gritstone that could at a distance be mistaken for man-made hill-forts. Rowtor Rocks, overlooking the village of Birchover, is a ridge of gritstone 240ft long and rising in places to 150ft. On nearby

Harthill Moor, Cratcliffe Tor and Robin Hood's Stride are similar ridges. At either end of the Stride, about 66ft apart, rise great monoliths called Inaccessible and Weasel. From a distance, especially when approached along the road from Winster, they look like the chimneys of a Tudor mansion, which is why the Stride is known unofficially as 'Mock Beggar's Hall'. Alport Stone, below the summit of the National Trust's Alport Hill (1,032ft) just outside the south-eastern tip of the Park, is a more isolated monolith much favoured by embryo rock climbers, too many of whom have celebrated their successful ascents by carving their initials on its face. Strangers sometimes take the Stone to have been erected by man, but it is a natural pillar of rock that has with-stood the weathering that has removed the rest of the ridge, and the Cat Stone, Cork Stone and Andle Stone, all on Stanton Moor, can be accounted for in the same way. Into these latter two stones, some unknown benefactor has firmly fitted metal rungs which provide, literally, easy steps to learning rock climbing. On the other side of the 15ft high Andle Stone is carved a memorial to the Duke of Wellington and to Lt Colonel William Thornhill, member of a local family, who fought with the Duke at the battles of Assaye in 1803 and Waterloo.

The name 'Andle' is interesting. It probably derives—like the various Anvil Stones around Britain—from the Saxon god Aigle, who reputedly threw stones that humans were powerless to move. The Eagle Stone on Baslow Edge must have acquired its name from the same source, for the true Peakrill pronounces 'eagle' as if it begins with an 'A'. Certainly this weathered monolith, which the young men of Baslow traditionally had to climb to prove their eligibility for marriage, bears no resemblance to that noble bird of prey. But there are rocks on Curbar Edge that do look like various birds and animals, the Seal Stones (1,978ft) on Seal Edge, near Kinder Scout, resemble seals, and from certain angles

38

one can see how the Wheel Stones—on Derwent Edge just south of the equally aptly named Salt Cellar and Cakes of Bread—acquired their local name of the Coach and Horses. Most remarkable of all is Toad's Mouth Rock, alongside the A625 close to Surprise View above Hathersage. It truly deserves its name, especially since some unknown artist has improved on nature by adding an eye to it.

Weathering also accounts for other oddly shaped rocks that abound on the gritstone, despite the usual attributions to Robin Hood, the devil and sundry giants practising their variations of shot-putting. Some of the most impressive of these are the various rocking stones, such as the one on Howden Mor, above the infant Derwent, and another farther to the north-east on Meltham Moor, just east of the Pennine Way. Rowtor Rocks has several rockable stones, but the best of them all, it is said, was toppled from its pivot stone by a gang of local youths on Whit Sunday 1799, which is worth mentioning to make the points that vandalism is no twentieth-century innovation and that memories live long in the Peak.

The shales, which might be expected to be less spectacular than the gritstones, provide two of the most dramatic natural features of the Peak: Mam Tor, the so-called 'shivering mountain', which frowns down on the village of Castleton, and Alport Castles (SK 128911), further north, which should not be confused either with Alport Stone or with the attractive village of Alport at the confluence of the Lathkill and Bradford rivers. Both Mam Tor and Alport Castles are escarpments in which the grits of the upper parts are being undermined by the weathering away of the softer shales below. On Mam Tor these upper portions are constantly falling, creating the shivering effect that made it one of the original 'wonders of the Peak' and making it totally unsuitable for climbing. At Alport Castles, which does at a distance look like a ruined castle, a large part of the rock is slowly pushing out from the face, rather as plaster sometimes bulges out from a wall. As it moves it pushes quantities of earth in front of it down into the valley below.

The shale valleys provide less drama but plenty of a quieter, more restful beauty. Especially where they are mixed with a little alluvium from the rivers, they supply a deep, heavy soil underlying narrow patches of rich green along the valleys of the Noe in Hope Dale, the Derwent around Darley Dale and Rowsley, and along the lower Wye, offering a striking contrast to the darker hills around them and adding yet another element to the variety of Peak scenery.

3   FIGURES IN A LANDSCAPE

IT is not always easy to decide just how much of the landscape is entirely natural and how much has been altered
by man. Take the peat moors of the northern Peak, for
instance. Nothing could appear more natural than these
boggy wastes with their covering of cotton grass and bilberry.
But modern techniques of pollen analysis hint that even here
man has altered his environment.

Vast quantities of tree pollen have been found in the peat,
indicating that this now virtually barren ground was once
forest. Changes in the species of the trees have been attributed
to climatic changes at various periods, which is still accepted
as being broadly true. But one rather odd factor has caused
some reservations among recent researchers. This is the
marked decline of elm pollen about 3000 BC. It could be just
another climatic variation, but what has shaken this belief is
the sudden increase of grass pollen from the same period,
which happens to have been about the same time that man
was abandoning his hunting economy in favour of agriculture.

The modern theory is that man selectively felled the elm
as a fodder plant for his cattle and sheep, and that the
increase in grass pollen indicates some fairly intensive
clearance of other trees. The amount of tree pollen found in
the peat declines steadily from this time onwards, but Dr J.
Tallis, of Manchester University, has found charcoal in the
peat, which he dates at about AD 1300, a time when man was
beginning to make intensive attacks on Britain's wildernesses.
Burning and draining may have been employed then in an

attempt to cultivate the High Peak. So it begins to look now as if the cotton grass and bilberry vegetation is the product of man's attempt to nurture rather than of 'nature undefiled'.

Those early farmers who hacked down the elms were not the first inhabitants of the Peak, but they were probably the first to leave a permanent mark on the landscape. Much earlier than that—perhaps around 9000 BC, though archaeologists are understandably reluctant to give precise dates—men certainly occupied a group of caves in the Magnesian Limestone at Cresswell Crags, on the Derbyshire–Nottinghamshire border about twelve miles east of the Peak. The few finds from that period—quartzite tools in a cave at Harborough Rocks, near Brassington, a flint from Ravenscliffe Cave in Cressbrook Dale and another in a field at Hopton—are just sufficient to show that Palaeolithic (Old Stone Age) man at least occasionally visited the area.

The first inhabitants of the Peak may have taken up residence in Mesolithic (Middle Stone Age) times around 5000–4000 BC. They have been a little more liberal in leaving their litter around, mostly in caves such as Thor's Cave in the Manifold Valley, where a schoolboy made some interesting finds in 1973. Many of their tools were of black chert—a siliceous rock similar in character to flint—which is found on the slopes of the Manifold and Wye valleys. Yet traces of these hunting folk are much less numerous in the limestone dales and uplands than on the lower spurs and foothills of the gritstone uplands from the Hope Valley northwards.

The reverse is true of the Neolithic (New Stone Age) immigrants. These first pastoralists arrived mostly from the west sometime between 4000 and 3000 BC, had settled mainly on the limestone uplands, where the light, well-drained soils and sparser woodlands were suitable for the domestic stock they brought with them and for such primitive arable farming as they may have practised around their long log-cabins. Some time later another, smaller, wave of immigrants reached the

Peak from the east. These were the ethnic group known as the Peterborough people, who evidently penetrated as far west as High Wheeldon, where traces of their pottery have been found in a cave. They were heavily built people with broad heads and stocky frames; the prototypes, it has been suggested, of the cartoonists' John Bull. They were traders whose feet gradually beat out trade routes across the Peak, along which they carried flints from Norfolk and stone axes from North Wales, the Lake District and Cornwall. Is it fanciful to see them as the primeval forerunners of the 'nation of shopkeepers'?

There was undoubtedly a fusion of these various people and the earlier settlers, whose more primitive culture may have lingered on for some time alongside the newer ways of life. As Sir Charles Fox pointed out: 'In the Lowlands of Britain new cultures of continental origin tend to be *imposed* on the earlier . . . culture. In the Highlands, on the other hand, these tend to be absorbed by the older culture'. The result is a greater continuity of culture, something that you become very aware of in the Peak District, where a custom like well dressing may be as old as the first traces of man on the hills.

The Neolithic agriculturists were the first people to make their mark on those hills, but it is not so much the evidence of their lives we see today on the limestone uplands as of their deaths. They buried their dead communally in chambered barrows. These megalithic tombs—so called because of the use of massive stones—are scattered widely across the White Peak. Inside them have been found bones of men, women and children, as well as of animals, along with flint arrowheads and sometimes fragments of pottery.

One of the best-preserved tombs is Five Wells on Taddington Moor (SK 124710), which at 1,400ft is the highest sited megalithic tomb in England. It consisted originally of two chambers inside a bell-shaped mound perhaps twenty feet high and was approached along passages between upright stones, some of which remain. Unfortunately the tumulus has been robbed of many of its stones, including the capstones. Other megalithic tumuli have been similarly rifled, but the one at Minninglow near Aldwark (SK 209573) probably less so than most, though traces of its passages have virtually gone. Similar in layout to Five Wells, it stands impressively, close to another barrow, within a clump of forlorn dying trees on a prominent hill above an almost bare plateau. Long Low near Wetton above the Manifold (SK 112540) is unique hereabouts in consisting of two mounds nearly 600ft apart linked by a long bank built over a drystone wall. Irregular depressions in adjacent fields may indicate the source of the stones.

Incidentally, the Peak District 'low', is, paradoxically, high. The word comes from the Old English *hlaw*, a hill or mound, usually in the Peak surmounted by an ancient monument, of which the Arbor Low stone circle (SK 160635) is the most impressive and the most evocative.

Much work has been done on Arbor Low, but many questions have yet to be conclusively answered. Opinions about its date, for instance, have changed slightly over the years. It used to be accepted as the work of the Bronze-Age Beaker People, who arrived in the area from the east around 1600 BC, and was thought to date from about 1500 BC. Some archaeologists are now inclined to push its date back to late Neolithic times, say 2000 to 1700 BC. Even its purpose remains in doubt, though it is generally accepted that it was the venue of some sort of ritual watched perhaps by spectators from the surrounding mound 50ft above the general ground level with a ditch 10ft deep between the mound and the grassy platform that holds the stone circle. Unless—and the hypothesis seems equally valid—the mound was intended to keep prying eyes from seeing whatever strange ceremony was enacted within the stone sanctuary.

Clearly, whatever did go on there must have had some

relationship to what occurred at Stonehenge or Avebury; the sites have much in common. But if you go up on to the bleak, almost treeless limestone plateau, 1,230ft above sea level, expecting another Stonehenge or Avebury you may be disappointed. The circle is much smaller—230ft in diameter—and all forty stones in the circle and the one in the centre have either fallen or were never upright, which is another unsolved mystery. Perhaps because it is less spectacular, and therefore less crowded with coach parties than the better known Wiltshire monuments, I find it more moving. It is possible on a weekday to be up there alone in the wind that always blows across the grassy plateau and to have an unbroken view of the barrows that cluster thickly around, including Gib Hill, the largest round barrow in the Peak. The past suddenly seems very close.

The Bull Ring at Dove Holes (SK 078782) is similar to Arbor Low in size, date and purpose, but far less evocative, partly because of its less isolated position but mainly because its stones have gone.

Nineteenth-century writers tended to attribute Dove Holes, Arbor Low and all Peakland's stone circles to the Druids and to hint at weird practices, including human sacrifice. Human sacrifice certainly cannot be ruled out; the skeleton of a man lying fully extended and without the grave goods that would have eased his passage into the next world was excavated at Arbor Low in 1902. But the stone circles, and the round barrows that are so plentiful on the limestone and rather scarcer on the gritstone, are known to have been the work of various Bronze-Age or earlier folk, though that is not to say that the over glamourised Druids may not have used them later, or, as rumour has it, that they have not been used for the practice of black magic in recent years.

The various Bronze-Age cultures are broadly distinguishable by their differing burial customs, though complications are caused by the fusion of cultures already mentioned. Single graves sometimes bear evidence of two distinct cultures, and to add to archaeological confusion some early barrows were later reopened for secondary burials. The picture that emerges rather mistily from the distant past is of the introduction to the Peak of the concept of burial in single graves in which were placed tall drinking vessels: the beakers after which their makers came to be known. These Beaker People tended to be round-headed—as distinct from the long-headed Neolithic folk—and skilled in the working of flint tools.

The Food Vessel People who followed them into the Peak probably came from a generally more culturally advanced group of the same stock, though the food vessels they interred with their dead were of coarser workmanship than the beakers they replaced. On the other hand, their flint axes were of high quality and their bronze implements were an innovation in the Peak. Nearly all the bronze tools found in the area came from Ireland, and the various necklaces and single beads of Whitby jet that have been found in some of their forty or so excavated barrows is further evidence that the Food Vessel People had quite extensive trade links. Primarily, however, they were pastoralists, like their predecessors, though they seem to have developed the cultivation of grain—probably barley—and for that reason indulged in deliberate but small-scale clearance of woodland.

This peaceful primitive rural life was rudely interrupted between about 1400 and 1000 BC by the arrival—again from the east—of spear-carrying invaders who overran the Peak and possibly enslaved the Food Vessel communities on whom they imposed an alien culture. Funeral customs changed again, the newcomers introducing cremation. The ashes of the dead were placed inside a large urn that was then put into a stone cist under a mound of earth, or sometimes in an existing barrow. These Urn People, as archaeologists label them, probably speeded the process of cultivation and clearance and certainly spread out in the quest for living space—perhaps encouraged by a change in climate—beyond the limestone country and on to the gritstone, where their barrows and stone circles are spread comparatively thickly along the edges and across the wild moors.

Of these stone circles, Wet Withins on Eyam Moor (SK 226790) is the largest. Ninety-five feet in diameter and consisting of sixteen upright stones inside a low circular bank, it is surrounded by smaller circles in an area rich in barrows, not all of which have been excavated.

Indeed the barrows of this period tend to be clustered together in what amount to cemeteries. A good place to see them is Stanton Moor, which has been said to have more prehistoric sites within its single square mile than any other area of its size in Britain. If the assertion is open to doubt, the fact remains that there are more than seventy barrows on the Moor. None is particularly spectacular; some indeed look to the untrained eye like natural bumps in the ground. But barrows they are and most of them have been excavated by two splendid local archaeologists: the late J. C. Heathcote and his son J. P. Heathcote, whose private museum in nearby Birchover is a treasure house of relics from the Moor and the surrounding district.

Some burials took place inside stone circles on Stanton Moor and neighbouring Harthill Moor. One of the best-preserved circles on Stanton Moor, the Nine Ladies (SK 248636), has a small cairn in its centre. The Ladies themselves are nine upright stones enclosed within a stone and earth bank some ninety-nine feet in diameter. About the same distance southwards stands a single upright stone called the King's Stone.

Nine seems to have been a significant number hereabouts. Another stone circle not far to the west on Harthill Moor is called Nine Stones (SK 227625), though only four large standing stones remain. Evidence of cremation has been found there.

Near the north-western edge of Harthill Moor a series of earthworks cover an area, oval in shape, of ¾ acre. Though so close to the numerous Bronze-Age monuments, it belongs to a later culture. Castle Ring, as it is called, is one of a dozen or so hill-forts in the Peak District that were constructed not earlier than the fifth century BC, when iron was introduced, rather belatedly, into the area. These were built as defensive sites on commanding hill-top positions, usually fortified with ramparts, ditches and counterscarp banks, and almost all on gritstone or shale, which suggests a marked change in the pattern of settlement.

Who built them and why? To those questions there is, as yet, no conclusive answer, so few having been thoroughly excavated. But there is enough evidence to suggest they were used for several centuries before, and during, the Roman occupation; perhaps even later in some cases, though it has been suggested that as peace came to the Peak they became cattle enclosures rather than military sites, an idea which has been shaken by a recent theory that the Carl Wark fort was not even constructed before about AD 500–600.

Carl Wark is certainly an improbable cattle enclosure. Standing 1,250ft above sea level on Hathersage Moor just to the east of the A625 (SK 260815), it has been described as 'among the most spectacular and easily accessible forts in this country'. Accessible to the visitor that is; it could hardly have been accessible to invaders. On three sides they would have had to scale an almost perpendicular cliff before being confronted with walls of massive gritstone boulders. The more exposed western side was protected for its full length of 150ft by a gritstone wall 10ft high, backed by a 20ft wide turf rampart.

But Carl Wark covers a mere 2 acres of ground; the Mam Tor fort has 16 acres enclosed within its rampart, ditch and counterscarp bank. The Mam Tor hill-fort is the largest in the Peak, and probably the most rewarding to visit, not least for the magnificent views it offers on all sides from its superb position 1,600ft above sea level, commanding the vales of Hope and Edale—1,000ft below—from the top of the 'shivering mountain'. The bank and ditch on the south-east and south-west sides have slithered away with these shivers of shale, but elsewhere they are well preserved. Although the fort is approached up steep slopes on all sides, the defenders left little to chance. The top of the rampart is 30ft above the bottom of the ditch in places, and the entrances are no more than narrow passages where the ramparts are turned inwards.

The other forts are less impressive, though Fin Cop, on the limestone above Monsal Dale (SK 175710) covers more than 10 acres, and Combs Moss, near Chapel-en-le-Frith (SK 055783) sits superbly on a gritstone headland 1,400ft above sea level. Burr Tor, above Great Hucklow (SK 180783), now lies on the landing ground of the Derbyshire and Lancashire Gliding Club. Other sites may still be discovered. A small fort at Ball Cross, on an escarpment overlooking Bakewell from the east (SK 228691), was identified by J. Stanley around 1950 and excavated by a party of Stockport Grammar School boys under his direction. They found that a stone rampart had been deliberately overturned, possibly by the Romans, and they also unearthed Iron-Age pottery and querns for grinding corn.

Numerous rotary querns of this period have been found around the Peak, probably originating from a large factory at Wharncliffe, north of Sheffield on the edge of the Park. Iron arrow-heads, swords, daggers and shields have been discovered, usually in barrows, but the best collection of Iron-Age material came from a cave at Harborough Rocks, which, like other Derbyshire caves, was occupied throughout the Romano–British period and even later. Daniel Defoe found a family living apparently quite happily in a cave in that same area— possibly in the same cave—in the 1720s. Almost within living memory workers in the limestone quarries round Buxton

49

were living in three- or four-room artificial caves hewn out of the hardening waste from the lime kilns.

Certainly cave-dwelling—either from choice or for protection—was common during the Roman occupation. The Brigantes, who settled in the Peak in the second century BC, were a warlike people who may have given the Romans an uncomfortable time at first with guerrilla warfare based on their cave hideouts, retreating to their hill-forts in times of crisis. Were they indeed the fort builders? It seems likely, though nobody is quite sure.

The Romans, despite a period of occupation as long as the time which separates us from the Civil War, left little lasting impression on the landscape of the Peak. Neither climate nor terrain was conducive to the building of villas. The warm springs of Buxton (Aquae Arnemetiae) attracted the growth of a small settlement which probably served as a leave centre for troops stationed in the area, but its only traces are in Buxton Museum; the two Roman baths excavated in the seventeenth and eighteenth centuries having been destroyed. Some lead mines were certainly exploited during the occupation—and probably earlier—but there is nothing stronger than local tradition to tell us which mines. Otherwise there are only the roads and the remains of two small forts to remind us of more than three centuries of Roman occupation.

Even the roads are mostly easier to follow on the map than on the ground. One ran more or less on the line of the present A515 as far as the Bull I' Th' Thorn inn at Hurdlow, apparently heading south-east for the fortified camp at Derventio, which is now Little Chester, an inner suburb of Derby. Close to the inn the modern road trends to the south-west towards Ashbourne. The Roman road continues its straight course and can be intermittently traced as far as Minninglow, where it vanishes even from the map. A more important road, thought to date from the arrival of Agricola in AD 77–8—some six years after the earliest penetration of

Page 51 Dovedale,
near Dove Holes

Page 52 (above) Upper Lathkill Dale. This part of the dale is usually dry; (below) Toad's Mouth Rock, above Hathersage, gritstone sculptured by natural weathering

the Romans into the Peak—ran from Ermine Street in the east to Watling Street in the west. From Littleborough, on the Trent in Nottinghamshire, it continued to Sheffield, and on to Brough, the site of the small fort of Navio. From there it followed a north-westerly course to another fort, now called Melandra, a mile west of Glossop above the east bank of the Etherow, and then continued out of the area to Manchester and on to join Watling Street at Chester. Portions of this road, known at least since 1627 as Doctor's Gate—apparently after a now otherwise forgotten Dr Talbot—can still be seen on its far-from-straight 16 mile course between Brough and Melandra, and another $1\frac{1}{2}$ miles lies under the A57 Snake Pass road.

Batham Gate is a little easier to follow, in places at least. This was the road from Buxton to Brough, where it joined the more important east-west road after climbing to 1,451ft on crossing Bradwell Moor. A Roman milestone found in 1862 at Silverlands, near to the southern end of this road to the baths, is now in Buxton Museum.

The forts themselves are not spectacular by archaeological standards. Brough covers only 2 acres, which is much less than most Roman auxiliary forts north of the Trent, suggesting that its permanent garrison was less than a cohort of 500 men. It was built about AD 158 on the site of an earlier Roman fort that had been abandoned for some reason about thirty years before, and was then continuously occupied for a further two centuries. Melandra was bigger, but was occupied for no more than approximately seventy years from around AD 80, its garrison being withdrawn about AD 140 presumably for service farther north. Since then its site has suffered at the hands of amateur archaeologists, vandals and the Home Guard of World War II who dug trenches across it to the confusion of more recent archaeologists.

But what is making Melandra an exciting fort is not so much its early history as what has happened—and is still happening—to it in the 1970s. In 1972 the town council of Glossop bought the 19 acre site, and with the excellent co-operation of the Melandra Field Group of archaeologists and of residents on the near-by Gamesley overspill estate, set to work on landscaping the site and turning it into a tourist attraction, where visitors will be able to see the outline of the fort and, it is hoped, bring additional revenue and employment to a town whose traditional textile trade has declined.

The Anglian settlement of the Peak was well established by around the middle of the seventh century. What had happened in the intervening 250 years or so between the departure of the Romans and the arrival of the new settlers is pure conjecture. The inhabitants—probably a mixture of races who can be conveniently described as Romano-British —made little impact on the landscape, though a settlement site and 'Celtic fields' at Blackwell, near Taddington, ½ mile south-west of Miller's Dale railway station (SK 131731), could belong to this period. So, too, could the fine example of terraced cultivation at Horse Stead, Priestcliffe, 1 mile to the east of the 'Celtic fields', and consisting of 13 terraces running north–south at about 1,000ft on an outcrop of toadstone. Several other examples of terraced cultivation around the Peak are more likely to be medieval lynchets, but the element of uncertainty adds to the attraction of trying to 'read' the landscape.

In an age of moon landings and computers there is a certain satisfaction in knowing that there is no stronger evidence than what the excellent HMSO guide to the Peak National Park describes as 'general historical probability' to ascribe two puzzling linear earthworks to the Dark Ages. Grey Ditch (SK 177815) cuts the ridge of Bradwell Edge and dives down the slope towards Bradwell Brook, reappearing beyond Batham Gate. Or rather—and this is from where one of its mysteries stems—it probably did; today it is in three sections and it is just possible that its builders relied on the steepness of the scarp slope and left that section untouched. The earthwork itself consists of a rampart roughly eight feet high and twenty-one feet wide at its base. Its purpose would be to block the northern entrance into Bradwell Dale from the north. The second earthwork, the Bar Dyke at Bradfield (SK 146643), is very similar in construction, but faces north-west and apparently guards a ridgeway. Both earthworks have considerable ditches on the northern, or northern-western, sides, posing questions about who built them against whom, to which there is no known answer.

Whoever was the expected enemy it could hardly have been the Angles, who either came from the lowlands to the east or, more usually, approached from the south, working their way first along the valleys of the Trent and then of its tributaries the Derwent and the Dove. The pattern of placenames in south Derbyshire shows this trend clearly. Anglo-Saxon place-name endings—especially the Old English *tun* 'farmstead village'—abound along the valleys and spread northward into the Peak along the Dove valley to Tissington and Hartington.

But the main Peakland river valleys were not generally suitable for immediate settlement because they were either too narrow or too thickly wooded. So the colonists climbed up on to the higher ground of the limestone uplands in search of settlement sites which provided space, a light, easily work-able soil, reasonable shelter from the wind and, above all, adequate water supply from springs or shallow wells. They found what they wanted in places like Brassington and Carsington, Kniveton, Hopton and Hognaston. Taddington, more than 1,000ft above sea level and near to the limit of cultivation in the Peak, is a more surprising choice for a fairly early Anglian settlement, though the wealth of prehistoric sites around suggest that this high ground above the Wye valley had its attractions for even earlier settlers.

But none of these Peakland settlements belongs to the very

earliest phase of Anglo-Saxon colonisation. In fact there is a complete absence in Derbyshire—and in the parts of adjacent counties that form the Peak—of the early Old English *-ingas* and *-ingaham* placename endings. Archaeologists have found no trace of Anglo-Saxon remains in the area earlier than the middle of the sixth century. Even the indefatigable Victorian, Thomas Bateman, who left hardly a barrow undisturbed within reach of his home at Middleton-by-Youlgreave, could find nothing earlier, though he did turn up numerous pagan Saxon secondary burials. His most exciting find was at Benty Grange (SK 146643), alongside the Roman road running south from Buxton. It contained the remains of an important Saxon warrior wearing chain-mail and a helmet of a type unique in Britain. Now in the Sheffield City Museum—along with the rest of the Bateman collection and other Peakland finds—it had over the nose-piece a silver Christian cross and on the crown the bronze figure of a boar, a pagan emblem; which suggests that this richly garbed chieftain was hedging his bets about the next world. This and other interesting graves hereabouts seem to date from around the early seventh century, a time, it has been suggested, when the Peak was disputed territory between the Mercian and Northumbrian kingdoms and being fought over by people of mixed Anglian and Celtic descent.

If this theory is correct—and nothing, as I say, is certain about this period—the settlement of the Derwent Valley may have begun a little later when more peaceful conditions were restored. The Old English element *leah,* 'wood or glade', tells its own tale of Anglo-Saxon settlement along the river and the clearance of woodland that went with it. Alderwasley, Lea, Darley, Wensley, Rowsley and Beeley are close neighbours along the valley, with Padley a little farther north.

It is from names like these that one catches the most revealing glimpse of the White Peak as it must have looked at that time. Ashbourne, Ashover, Ashleyhay, Ashford, Birchover,

Monyash and Youlgreave (the yellow grove) are placenames that paint a picture of a fairly thickly wooded countryside, with ash, then, as now, the most common tree, especially on the steep valley slopes. That such names are almost totally missing from the map of the Dark Peak does not indicate the absence of woodland but that there was little clearance, for reasons which will be explained in the next chapter.

Meanwhile, there is one place name that deserves a special mention. Wensley is derived from Wodensley, 'the glade devoted to (the worship of) Woden', suggesting a pre-Christian Anglo-Saxon settlement. Christianity came to Mercia in 653, when the Mercian King Penda's son, Peada, married the Christian daughter of King Oswy of Northumbria and brought back to his capital Hrewpandun (now Repton, in south Derbyshire) four priests, lead by Diuma, the first bishop of Mercia. From the monastery they founded there, these and other missionaries went out to preach. But perhaps even earlier in the same century the missionary priests who had kept Celtic Christianity alive in the north and west had spread their gospel as far south as the Peak from their head-quarters at Iona and Lindisfarne. By the end of the seventh century, preaching stones or crosses had begun to appear on the hills of the Peak. More than thirty survive. The finest, in the churchyards at Bakewell, Bradbourne and Eyam, are thought to date from the eighth century, and Sir Nickolaus Pevsner sees a Northumbrian derivation on the vine scrolls of Eyam cross, whch is the only one in the Peak that has retained its cross-head. Neither the Eyam cross nor the Bake-well one is in its original position; both were found on the hills in the neighbourhood, where others remain *in situ,* distributed fairly evenly between the limestone and the grit-stone. But all the Peak crosses are of gritstone, which is more tractable than limestone to cutting tools.

Significantly, these Peakland crosses date either from the eighth or early ninth centuries, or, more numerously, from

the tenth century; none from the later ninth century when
the threat of Viking invasion hung over the land.

Placename evidence suggests that this invasion was never
more than a threat in the Peak, though the wapentake of
Wirksworth, which covers the Low Peak is certainly Danish.
The lowlands and foothills to the east are rich in Scandinavian
placenames—Denby Dale and Upper Denby, Gunthwaite
and Thurgoland, Cutthorpe and Hardstoft, to name just a
few—but the Peak itself has a mere sprinkling. There is a
little group of Booths that form the northern part of what
became the parish of Edale, and Hathersage Booth, farther to
the east. West of the Derwent there is only Kettleshulme,
'Ketil's island', or water meadow; Winster, 'the winter
pasture'; the totally inexplicable Thorpe, 'secondary settlement', in the Dove Valley, far from any other Danish village;
and perhaps Flagg, sitting bleakly on the limestone plateau
nursing a strong local tradition that it was a Viking settlement
and retaining an unmistakable Danish influence until well
into the nineteenth century. An even stronger tradition maintains that Odin Mine, Castleton was worked for lead by the
Danes.

Even these scattered fragments of Danish territory may date
from the time when Saxon and Dane had learnt to live
together in comparative harmony to become one English
nation. By then the period of colonisation in the Peak was
almost over and the people of the area had settled down to
consolidate their holdings.

4 THE CHANGING LANDSCAPE

Acharacter from one of J. B. Priestley's splendid time plays who found himself carried back 900 years to spend Act II as a Norman invader marching across the Peak would have no great difficulty in finding his way around. There would be differences, of course, but at least most of the places would be the same even if their spellings had altered.

The Anglo-Saxons chose their settlement sites so skilfully that almost all were recorded in the Domesday Book and have survived to the present day. A few have changed their names, like the royal manor of Metesforde, which we know today as Matlock. A few others—very few compared with the villages in south Derbyshire and elsewhere on the grasslands of the East Midland 'Shires'—vanished in the medieval agrarian revolution when sheep rearing replaced arable farming. Nether Haddon, though its name still appears on the map, became virtually depopulated when the owner of Haddon Hall extended his park in the Middle Ages. A portion of Edensor (pronounced 'Ensor') was demolished in the eighteenth century because it marred the fourth Duke of Devonshire's view from his windows at Chatsworth, the remainder following in the nineteenth century during the reign of the sixth Duke who, being a more considerate man, had a new—and architecturally extraordinary—village built on a less offensive site. Two villages in the valley of the upper Derwent —Ashopton, and Derwent itself—disappeared under the waters of Ladybower Reservoir well within living memory.

To offset these losses a mere sprinkling of new settlements have been established since Domesday. Ambergate and the delightfully named Parsley Hay are products of the railway age. The New Mills that gave that place its name were corn mills established around 1500, though its importance sprang from the much later cotton mills. Cromford, on the other hand, though essentially an eighteenth-century cotton-mill village, has roots that go back at least to Domesday, when it was a berewick—probably no more than a farm building or two—of the royal manor of Wirksworth. But on the whole, the Domesday manors bear a close relationship to the modern towns and villages. This is strikingly illustrated by Offerton, a tiny hamlet on the steeply rising south bank of the Derwent overlooking Hathersage. In Domesday it was divided between the manors of Hope and Hathersage; it is still shared by these two parishes today. In size, too, it has remained almost static throughout 900 years, which is something that can also be said of a score or more Peakland settlements, including a group of hamlets farther up the Hope Valley: Hurst, Thornhill and Aston.

In another respect, though, Offerton differs from its neighbours. It faces north-east, whereas Hurst, Thornhill and Aston, like the few settlements in the Vale of Edale, face south to make the most of the sun in spring and summer, which seems to indicate a fair degree of sophistication amongst those Anglo-Saxon planners. All these hamlets belong to a late phase in the age of colonisation. The earlier settlers, with less regard for such subtleties, concentrated on building their homes where there was an adequate supply of water. This was not always easy to find on the porous limestone, but sometimes the water-table could be reached through fissures in the rock or was at a high level because of the presence of some impermeable igneous rock. Names like Bakewell, Blackwell, Tideswell and Bradwell speak for themselves, though Whatstandwell, which sounds like another of the same ilk, takes its name from a Walter Stonewell, who had a house adjoining the site where a bridge was built across the Derwent in 1393. Springs often emerge at the junction of limestone and shale, which accounts for such settlements as Elton, Grindlow, Great Hucklow and Great Longstone. On the gritstone there was no shortage of water, but the land was not hospitable for large-scale settlement.

On the limestone the shapes of the villages were determined either by the nature of the water supply or by the terrain. The characteristic limestone village is long and narrow, stretched out along the floor of a dry dale, like Stoney Middleton and Tideswell, or on a narrow shelf of level ground as at Eyam, Over Haddon and Wensley. But the most striking examples of these linear villages are Chelmorton and Taddington, which have retained their ancient forms intact despite some later infilling. In both villages the church is at the highest point. At 1,100ft Chelmorton Church is one of the highest-sited parish churches in England. It backs directly on to Chelmorton Low, rising above the level of cultivation; opposite is the Church Inn; below that the houses run down a gently sloping village street with the farms on either side in the pre-enclosure manner that is common enough in the Peak, where Parliamentary Enclosures came late, as most things tend to do in this strangely remote heart of England. Below the houses are the drystone walls enclosing narrow fields that have retained their medieval pattern. But more of that later. Here it will suffice to say that Taddington is a slightly less spectacular version of Chelmorton, dropping quite steeply down towards the valley of the Wye and a pre-World War II bypass that carries the A6 up Taddington Hill below the village.

The nucleated village, built round a large green, which is so characteristic of Northumberland and County Durham, is much less common in the Peak. The best example is Monyash, where the houses cluster round a cross-roads, church, inn and green, with a pond, or mere, at the heart. It was clearly a place of some importance at one time, perhaps even before it became a lead-mining centre. Tissington and Foolow have similar arrangements of pond and greens without this suggestion of past importance which is found again at Hartington. But while Monyash sits rather bleakly on the uplands, Hartington has a valley setting with the hills rising steeply on three sides.

Valley settlements, except along the Derwent, are not numerous in the Low Peak owing to lack of space. There is just enough room for clusters of houses and steeply rising fields at Crowdecote and Mill Dale on the Dove and a little more space in the angle between Manifold and Dove—just before the confluence—for a slightly larger settlement at Ilam. Bakewell and Ashford are the only settlements on the Wye before the hills close in to form a deep gorge. Above that there is only the tiny hamlet of Miller's Dale. The Lathkill and Bradford rivers are similarly devoid of settlements, except for Alport at their confluence.

On the gritstone and shale, where water was plentiful, settlement tended to be more dispersed, though naturally in the High Peak a valley site was more generally favoured. The traditional 'Celtic' scattered pattern of highland settlement with no real village centre—so frequently encountered in Devon and Cornwall—is rare in the Peak except on the western moors, where such places as Quarnford and Fawfieldhead fall into this category, though Edale may have originated in this way. The East Moor, because of its boggy soil has probably always been thinly populated as it is today.

Indeed our Priestleyan traveller in Norman England would have found Peakland most sparsely inhabited. W. G. Hoskins has estimated the entire population of England in 1086 at $1\frac{1}{4}$ million. Probably no more than about 2,000 of them lived in the Peak, much less than in modern Wirksworth.

However, the parishes into which the area came to be

divided were often enormous. In the more populous East Midlands, where the soil was good, the parishes were roughly circular in shape and fairly small. with the houses at the centre. The late Sir Dudley Stamp estimated the average lowland Midland parish as covering about 4 sq miles, or 2,560 acres. In the Peak, with its thin soil and sparse population, far more land was required. Hartington was divided into four quarters: Upper, Middle, Nether and Town Quarters, stretching some 16 miles from Buxton down to Alsop-en-le-Dale, and these quarters are still named on the map, although other parishes have now been formed within them. Ashover still covers 11,000 acres. The ecclesiastical parish of Bakewell —the only place in the Peak with two priests mentioned in Domesday Book—was 20 miles long and an average of 8 miles wide as late as the 1880s, when it had 9 chapelries and 14 townships under its wing. Further north, Hope had the only church mentioned in Domesday in the Derbyshire portion of the High Peak, and at the end of the last century the parish still covered 38,400 acres, though its population was just under 2,000. Much of its acreage was unoccupied grouse moor.

At the time Domesday Book was compiled what is now Hope parish was part of the King's Forest of the High Peak, which contained some 180 sq miles in the extreme north-west of Derbyshire. It is bounded in the north by the river Etherow, on the east by the Derwent, on the south by the Wye from its source at Buxton, and on the west by the Goyt. It was divided into three wards: Campana (open country), Hope and Long-dendale, the latter being described in Domesday as 'waste'.

This was forest in the strict dictionary sense of 'unenclosed woodland district kept for hunting', or, as one Richard fitz Nigel defined it, 'the safe dwelling place of wild beasts, not of every sort, but of the sort that dwell in the woodlands, not in any sort of place, but in certain places suitable for the purpose'. Thickly wooded it was in places, but with stretches of wild, open country. And its 'wild beasts'—wolves, boar, deer especially—were not safe from Saxon or Danish kings and perhaps even less so from the Norman Angevin kings who imposed a strict code of forest laws administered by the peripatetic justices in Eyre north of the Trent to ensure that the pleasures of the chase and the kill were reserved for their own royal delight.

'In the forests', to quote Richard fitz Nigel again, 'are the secret places of the kings and their great delight. To them they go for hunting, having put off their cares, so that they may enjoy a little quiet. There, away from the continuous business and incessant turmoil of the court, they can for a little time breathe in the grace of natural liberty, wherefore it is that those who commit offences there lie under the royal displeasure alone.'

Those who did incur the royal displeasure appeared either before the two great courts held annually at Tideswell, or at the lesser courts—Swainmotes—held not more than three times a year at various places, and attended by the steward of the forest and not less than twenty foresters. In addition to these courts, the foresters met every three weeks to exchange information and hear complaints. The Forest Charter of 1217, that eased to some extent the severity of previous laws, made it clear that punishments for poaching were imposed on a strictly hierarchical basis; a freeman who hunted the royal deer lost his freedom; a villein lost his right hand; a serf lost his life. But in fact in the High Peak Forest the courts were merciful. 'No case of capital punishment' is recorded in the Rolls of the Forest, according to I. E. Burton, who searched them for his book *The Royal Forest of the Peak,* 'and most of the offenders were let off with moderate fines: only in the worst cases, when violence had been used against the King's officers, was imprisonment inflicted'.

With the death in 1307 of Edward I, the last king to take an active interest in preserving the forest, the Charter gradually fell into disrepute. Poaching increased. Encroachments along the fringes of the forest became more numerous. Raiding parties cut down the oak, birch and fir in Longden-dale and used them—surprisingly perhaps in an area so rich in building stone—in the construction of their houses within the bounds of the old forest. The woods of Hope and other places in the vicinity were similarly 'wasted', and other parts of the forest were attacked in much the same way. The Wars of the Roses and the increasing demands of the lead smelters for fuel made conservation even more difficult. By the end of the fifteenth century little of the Royal Forest was left to conserve, and efforts by the first two Tudor monarchs to restore the old forest laws and impose fines for encroachment met with little success. The Civil War, so destructive of trees nationally, ravaged the forest not only of its remaining timber but also of its few remaining deer. In the reign of Charles II the Royal Forest ceased to exist even technically.

Two other royal forests on the fringes of the Peak had similar histories. Macclesfield Forest, in the west, exists today as a large stretch of pine woods almost surrounding the village of the same name. Duffield Frith, in the extreme south, is still thickly wooded along the west bank of the Derwent, where Shining Cliff Woods, now owned by the National Trust, have been replanted since World War I. But this is a fraction of a forest which as late as 1560 still had a circuit of more than thirty miles. There still stood then 112,000 oaks along with underwood which included white and black thorn, hazel, holly, maple, crab-tree and the alder from which the village of Alderwasley took its name. But the hunger of the local furnaces for timber for smelting was such that only 27 years later a mere 6,000 oaks survived, and by 1650 nothing was left but the name of 'the late disafforested Forest or Chase called Duffield Frith'.

Today isolated farms with such names as Mansell Park, Bradley Park, Wildpark and Daypark stand on the site of the fenced enclosures within the park that were set aside for the protection of the royal deer. Ravensdale Park has indeed survived in an attenuated form as an enclosed piece of woodland. Names like Openwoodgate, Bargate, Wardgate and Cowers (once Cowhouse) Lane mark the course of roads through the forest, and the village of Hulland Ward takes its name from one of the four wards into which the forest was divided. The original chapel of the foresters still survives, though much restored, as St John's, Belper. A similar chapel built by foresters in the High Peak about 1225 was replaced by a larger church on the same site in the fourteenth century but it gave its name to what is now the small town of Chapel-en-le-Frith (in the forest), which was formerly called Bowden. Just east of Chapel, the village of Peak Forest stands in an ironically bare stretch of country, but Chamber Farm here may mark the site of a building in which forest courts were held.

Another link with the forest is ruined Peveril Castle, overlooking the village of Castleton. Established by William the Conqueror to control the wild High Peak, its early custodians also held the office of Keeper of the Royal Forest and the Plantagenet kings used it as a hunting box. All that is left of the original castle in which Henry II received the submission of Malcolm, King of Scotland, in 1157 is a curtain wall—partly of herring-bone masonry—on a site that would be almost unassailable on three sides even today. The keep, nearly 60ft high, was added in 1175. Today this impressive shell is the Peak's sole surviving contribution to medieval military architecture, though there are early castle mounds at Bakewell, Bradfield and Camp Green, Hathersage.

The clearance of woodland has probably changed the face of the Peak more than any other single factor since the Norman Conquest. It was a process that had been going on, as we have seen, for literally thousands of years before that, but in a small way, at least until the arrival of the Anglo-Saxon settlers. Using axe and fire they cleared much woodland from immediately around their buildings and grazing grounds, but it has been estimated that more than 30 per cent of Domesday Derbyshire was still under woodland; the proportion in the Peak was probably nearer 40 per cent. In 1949 the figure for Derbyshire was down to 4 per cent, compared with the national average of 6 per cent, and for the Peak it was probably lower still.

This denudation had many causes. As population grew so did the demand for agricultural land. Farmers felled the trees and the nibbling teeth of their sheep prevented regeneration. With the disappearance of the royal forests, those early 'national parks' where conservation had been practised for motives diametrically opposed to those of today, there was no further thought for the future. The demands of the navy had to be met even from woodland as far inland as the Peak; the demands of the smelters of lead and iron were even greater. By the end of the seventeenth century the holocaust of trees was so great that the local smelting mills were being fed by timber carried from Hertfordshire and other distant counties.

The eighteenth-century landowners did much to redress the balance. Sir Richard Arkwright is said to have planted 50,000 trees annually for 7 years in the Derwent valley around his Willersley estate. 'The vast woods' that Horace Walpole noted hanging down the hills at Chatsworth in 1760 must have been mature trees then, but certainly since the early eighteenth century successive dukes of Devonshire have planted many thousands of trees on their estates. The fifth Duke of Rutland planted extensively along the Wye Valley early in the nineteenth century, and other local landowners followed the dukes' lead, as they generally did in other matters. Planting became less fashionable in the second half of the nineteenth century, but by then the demands of the ship builders and smelters had diminished and the proportion of woodland continued to increase slightly nationally until two world wars compelled reliance on home-grown timber, causing a drastic depletion of mature trees.

During the last half century, however, renewed planting has had its effect on the appearance of the Peak despite the loss of several thousand trees on a wild night in February 1962. Some of this planting is the work of private owners, but a greater acreage has been planted by the Forestry Commission (established for that purpose in 1919), the water authorities responsible for the reservoirs, the National Trust and the Peak Park Planning Board. The aims of these bodies differ. The Forestry Commission's main purpose is to reduce the nation's economic and strategic dependence on overseas sources of timber. With its prime attention on the balance of payments rather than on the balance of beauty, it naturally plants more quick-growing conifers than the slower maturing deciduous trees. But the Commission has become increasingly sensitive to the appearance of the landscape and there is little talk today of 'soulless rows of pines'. The 1,500 acres that the Commission is planting on exposed land between 1,000– 1,500ft overlooking the Goyt is a good blending of various pines with deciduous trees round the fringes.

The water authorities have an eye to profit, which inclines them in favour of conifers, but that is not the main object of their tree-planting exercise. Their policy is to grow trees on their gathering grounds, and especially round their reservoirs, to prevent pollution from farming and people. Britons are attracted to water as wasps to a jam dish, and with results that could be equally unpleasant. Many Peakland reservoirs are accessible to the public, but usually in certain specific places where they can be observed and, if necessary, controlled. But the tree-planting policy has other important aims besides keeping control of animals, human and domestic. Trees hold water and thus tend to even out the heavy rainfall. They also do a useful job in helping to prevent soil erosion, especially on the steep slopes.

The Peak Park Planning Board like the National Trust is naturally much more concerned with the 'preservation and enhancement of natural beauty' than either of the other bodies can afford to be. The Board's forestry workers plant about 20,000 trees a year, and look after more than 600 acres of woodland as well as offering a forestry advisory service to farmers and other private owners of woodlands. The emphasis is on regeneration as much as planting; on the long-term appearance of the environment, so that much of the planting is of indigenous broad-leaved species, such as ash, lime, wych elm, rowan and birch. One especially pleasing feature of the Board's work, with an eye to the future, is the way in which it has managed to interest schools. A good deal of tree planting, especially in 1973—Tree Planting Year—has been carried out by schoolchildren with help from the Board.

On the whole, the various bodies, with their differing aims, achieve a reasonably harmonious blending and work closely together. The area will obviously never return to its thickly wooded early medieval state—few of us would want that anyway—but nor is it ever likely to look as bare as it must have done 200 years or so ago. It is an area of small, scattered woodlands—copses, shelter belts and hanging woods—though a drive over the western fringe of the limestone uplands along the A515 from Buxton as far south as Tissington gives a chilling picture of an almost treeless landscape. On the other hand, if you take the almost parallel A6 from Buxton along the valleys of the Wye and Derwent to Ambergate or beyond, you may get the impression that the Peak is exceptionally thickly and most beautifully wooded, with the stretch down Taddington Hill and past Shacklow Wood to Ashford-in-the-Water outstandingly beautiful. Farther north, in the High Peak, the drive past three great reservoirs—Howden, Derwent and Ladybower—may remind you of the scenery of a Scottish loch, with the thickly wooded hillside—mainly conifers but with a fringe of maple and rowan near the water's

E

edge—softening the harsh outlines of the steep gritstone slopes.

The reservoirs are relatively new features of the Peak landscape. In a sense they are parasites, for though some do supply water to parts of the area they were not built for that purpose. Just as much products of the Industrial Revolution as are the cotton mills of Glossop and Cromford, they were constructed to hold the water that would slake the thirst of the rapidly expanding populations of the north midland industrial conurbations. Sheffield, Manchester, Stockport, Huddersfield, Nottingham, Leicester and Derby, along with many smaller places, get much, if not all, their water from the High Peak.

The Sheffield Water Board, formed in 1830, was the first water authority to lift up its eyes unto the hills for its source of supply. In 1836 it completed the first Peakland reservoir, the Redmires Middle Reservoir on Hallam Moors. Within twenty more years the Upper and Lower Redmires and two Rivelin reservoirs were finished. Four more had been built in the area by the time Sheffield Corporation took over the Board's work in 1888. By then Manchester and other towns had joined in the rape of the Peak.

But the conquest was not achieved without sacrifices. On the night of 4 February 1852, after several days of exceptionally heavy rainfall, Bilberry Reservoir's embankment of earth, stone and puddled clay, undermined by springs, collapsed. More than 86 million gallons of water poured down into the Holme valley, sweeping away buildings and killing 81 people. In half an hour the reservoir was empty, damage estimated at £250,000 had been done, many people were homeless and more than 7,000 were thrown out of work owing to the destruction of several mills. An even worse disaster followed twelve years later when about midnight on 11 March 1864 a landslip caused the collapse of the embankment of the newly built Dale Dike Reservoir. Water which was gradually filling the reservoir swept down into the Loxley valley at a speed of 60 miles an hour. In what proved to be Britain's worst flooding disaster, 244 lives were lost and tremendous damage was done to property. The Sheffield Water Company paid £373,000 in compensation.

Despite these major setbacks, water authorities continued to look at the High Peak as an ideal gathering ground for their water supplies. In 1899 the corporations of Nottingham, Derby and Leicester joined with the Sheffield and various Derbyshire authorities to form the Derwent Valley Water Board, which promptly set to work to flood the upper Derwent and Ashop valleys and construct the largest and best-known chain of reservoirs in the Peak. Work began on Howden in 1901 and the reservoir was brought into use in 1912. Derwent Reservoir was opened in 1916 after fourteen years building. Ladybower, the largest, took only ten years to construct between 1935 and 1945, work continuing throughout the war.

Ladybower's vital statistics are breathtaking. It has a surface area of 504 acres, a perimeter of 13 miles and a maximum depth of 135ft. Its embankment, 1,250ft long, 665ft at the bottom tapering to 17ft thick at the top, contains 1 million tons of earth, 100,000 tons of concrete and 100,000 tons of clay. The *Manchester Guardian*, reporting its opening by King George VI on 25 September 1945, described it as 'the largest artificial reservoir formed by the construction of an earthwork embankment in the British Isles, if not in Europe'.

The three reservoirs can store together more than 10,000 million gallons of water, which sounds a most adequate amount until you reflect that our average daily consumption works out at around 50 gallons per head and that brewers use 350 gallons to brew 1 gallon of beer.

The construction of the Howden and Derwent reservoirs 'most rudely disturbed the amenities' of Ashopton and its immediate neighbourhood, as J. B. Firth remarked when he visited the area in 1905. A railway line from Bamford station

71

had been built to carry stones and other materials—almost all from local sources—across river and road at Ashopton 'by an ugly viaduct', and an embankment scarred the hillside. The assurance that this intrusion would be merely temporary, Firth feared, was 'too good to be true'. His scepticism was unjustified. The line was removed and can only be faintly traced in places today. Unfortunately—and Firth did not bargain for this—Ashopton and the neighbouring village of Derwent were also removed, or at least submerged under the waters of Ladybower. Among the 'amenities most rudely disturbed' was Derwent Hall, a typical Peakland manor house that had been built by the Balguy family in 1692 and later became a seat of the Duke of Norfolk. Its oak panelling was saved and now adds graciousness to the walls of the water authority's offices alongside the dam. A fine seventeenth-century packhorse bridge that stood close to the hall was taken down, stored, and later re-erected higher up the river Derwent at Slippery Stones. The spire of Derwent Church— or some three quarters of it—stuck out of the water like the periscope of a submarine but it became unsafe, and when visitors walked out to it in the exceptionally dry summer of 1959, the authorities decided to demolish it.

The building of the rather smaller reservoirs of Fernilee (completed in 1937) and Errwood (1967) to ease Stockport's thirst, involved the flooding of part of the Goyt Valley, alterations to roads, the removal of a packhorse bridge which had crossed the Wildmoorstone Brook near Goyts Bridge to a new site a mile upstream and the partial dismantling of Errwood Hall.

About these violations of the peace of the Peak there are two schools of thought. 'When rape is inevitable you may as well relax and enjoy it' runs an old saying which seems analogous with what is probably the majority view about these reservoirs. That many people find relaxation and enjoyment in contemplating these large stretches of placid water in lovely surroundings, there can be no doubt at all. When facilities can be offered for sailing, as at Errwood and Combs, the appeal is all the greater. Coach trips from surrounding towns 'to the dams' are well patronised; in high summer the road that runs alongside the Upper Derwent reservoirs is lined with cars, and it was the congestion in the Goyt Valley after the opening of Errwood reservoir that led to the now famous weekend traffic restrictions in that area. Undoubtedly these artificial lakes have added a new dimension to an area that lacked natural lakes, and have brought pleasure to many people—but mainly to those who cannot remember what was there before. They took away beauty as well as adding to it. Little of the land taken so far has been good for agriculture. Much of it has been of little good to anybody except to lovers of solitude and wild beauty; wilderness in fact. But wilderness is not easy to find in England now. Seventy-three sizable stretches of it in the Peak have now been lost under the water which covers 29 per cent of the national park. When you think about those 50 gallons per head per day, you may think it a fair exchange. Perhaps—but how much more wilderness can we afford to lose?

This is a problem that mainly affects the Dark Peak. The White Peak—the limestone—is dry except for occasional meres. These are ancient ponds fed by springs and enlarged to provide drinking ponds for cattle. Today, cattle are usually more hygienically watered from troughs with a piped supply and many meres are silting up, but fine examples remain at Hartington, Foolow, Monyash and Tissington. Now inhabited by ducks, these ponds are well maintained and likely to remain so, though one local councillor has suggested the conversion of Flagg Mere into a lorry-park as an 'amenity'. But there is another, less ancient, type of mere which is out-living its usefulness and may disappear from the landscape unless deliberately preserved by farmers with a feeling for history. Such meres, usually smaller than the village type, are numerous in the Monyash–Over Haddon district. They are rounded, frequently cement lined, and often mistakenly described as dew-ponds. In fact they are fed by surface water running from higher ground, or quite often when they stand hard by a roadside wall, by run-off from the road itself.

The drystone roadside walls, and those that separate one field from another, are the most distinctive and ubiquitous man-made features of the Peak scenery. Except above 1,500ft, where much of the land is unenclosed and a post-and-wire fence is good enough to separate one man's grouse moor from his neighbour's, and below 700ft, where some landowners prefer the hawthorn hedge, they mark off all boundaries, as well as controlling livestock movement and affording shelter to animals. More durable than either hedges or wooden fencing against any force except human vandalism, they will stand for half a century without attention and have the added merit of being built with material literally lying at hand. Indeed the building of a stone wall often served a dual purpose in that stone was being cleared from the land at the same time to make way for the plough.

These drystone walls are seen at their most spectacular as they climb precipitously out of the deeper, steeper dales to disappear into the blue, or stride seemingly endlessly across the gritstone moors. But you become most aware of them on the limestone uplands where they enclose neat little rectangular fields, or strikingly long narrow ones.

Most of these walls date from the age of enclosures which in the Peak was roughly between 1760 and 1830. Some are much older. 'The low drye stone walls round some ground' that Celia Fiennes noticed in 1697 were visible evidence of the gradual enclosure that had been going on for two centuries or more and was a product of the nationwide swing from arable farming to stock rearing, though some of the earliest walls in the Peak enclosed land that had probably never been under arable. These first mortarless walls simply divided one vast sheep run from another. As early as 1234 the *Annals of Dunstable* record the loss of 800 sheep 'of the flock belonging to Dunstable Priory' at Bradbourne, but 50 years later 'the Priory possessed a flock of sheep at Bradbourne numbering 1,200'. This may have been a comparatively small flock by Peak standards for another, unspecified, monastic owner had 5,500 sheep on one huge pasture.

The great religious houses were the principal sheep farmers, and many of them were exporting wool to Florentines and Flemings by the end of the thirteenth century. As the monasteries themselves were often far from the Peak the day-to-day management of these ranches was carried out, mainly by lay brothers, from isolated granges, a name derived from a medieval French word meaning granaries. Many of these purpose-built monastic farmhouses still survive in name, though most have been completely rebuilt. Few traces remain of the chapels in which the lay brothers worshipped at least twice daily, though one at Meadow Place Grange, near Over Haddon, survived as a farm building until the mid-nineteenth century. Some portions of Smerrill Grange, near Youlgreave, must have belonged to the original grange, and there are medieval outbuildings at Stanage Grange, near Newhaven, Harewood Grange, near Holymoorside—a possibly significant placename—and perhaps at Mouldridge Grange, Gratton Dale, and One Ash Dale, Monyash, which was an appendage of the Cistercian house of Roche Abbey in Yorkshire and where later John Bright, of the Anti-Corn Law League spent his honeymoon. Every grange had its own mere, and many of these survive today, with particularly good ones at Mould-ridge and One Ash.

Some monasteries owned more than one grange in the Peak. The Augustinian abbey of Darley, situated in what is now a northern suburb of Derby, had numerous granges round Wirksworth, of which at least four are still farmed today. Dunstable Priory held Mouldridge Grange as well as

the one at Bradbourne, and about 1200 the wealthy Premon-
stratensian house of Welbeck in Nottinghamshire acquired
four granges in the Upper Derwent Valley. These were
exceptional, though certainly not unique, in being on the
gritstone; the vast majority were on the limestone, and it is
on the central limestone uplands that most granges stand
today, nearly all mainly concerned with the rearing of cattle
rather than sheep.

Arable farming is comparatively rare in the Peak, and it
used to be held that open-field farming was not widely
practised in the area. Opinions have now changed as a result
of studies by W. E. Wightman and others. The pattern of
ridge and furrow, so familiar a sight on the Midland Plain,
was once stamped clearly around the villages even on the
limestone uplands and can still be seen around Tissington,
Thorpe and Fenny Bentley, and less distinctly elsewhere
below about 1,300ft. With a few exceptions, mostly in the
Wirksworth area where the land was too heavily pitted with
lead-mine workings to leave room for open-field farming—as
can still be seen north of Middleton-by-Wirksworth—it seems
that almost every village on the limestone had its open-field
system, though not necessarily on a three-field rotation.
Possibly there were one, two, three and even four-field systems
operating in different villages. Even some of the fifty or so
monastic granges had some unenclosed arable in strips,
though this development may have occurred under the new
ownership after the dissolution of the monasteries.

Some enclosure by agreement must have been going on
long before the eighteenth-century Enclosure Acts. Often
just a single strip of 220yd by 22yd was taken from the open
field and enclosed, which accounts for some of the long,
narrow fields enclosed by stone walls in places like Chelmorton, Litton and Wardlow. At Ible, a remote village
perched above the western end of the Via Gellia, Dr Wightman has found evidence of an enclosure formed by amalga-

mating four separate strips of this kind. The pattern of enclosure can often be fairly clearly seen in the limestone upland villages. The stone walls closest to the village probably enclosed the crofts behind the houses; the slightly curving walls beyond indicate the reversed 'S' shape of the medieval strips, and farther away still are the more regular-shaped fields of the seventeenth- and eighteenth-century enclosures.

Another type of enclosure that went on piecemeal from the Middle Ages onwards was the taking in of hitherto uncultivated land from the waste and woodland for the creation of new farms and fields. These intakes are quite numerous round Ashover, and there is an Intake Farm at Little Hucklow that presumably originated in this way.

Since the enclosures, the face of the Peak has changed surprisingly little, apart from the scars inflicted by quarrying. The canals simply scratched the cheeks, the broader slashes inflicted by the railways have now healed into long strips of green, and most of the area has escaped the wirescape of electricity pylons and overhead transmission lines. True, road, electrified railway and overhead power cables run side by side for several miles along Longdendale, but they are cut down to match-stick size against the high, wild valley sides, and for 3 miles between Woodhead and Dunford Bridge both the railway and the power lines burrow underground; the railway through a new tunnel, opened in 1954, and the power lines through the northernmost bore of the two earlier tunnels. This sensible arrangement cost the Central Electricity Generating Board nearly £2¾ million and its engineers 5 years' exacting work which they finally, splendidly, completed in October 1969, bringing immense pleasure to those discerning people who like their wilderness untrammelled by the trappings of modern civilisation.

5   NATURAL HISTORY

THERE are few places in the Peak where the sense of the past comes over more strongly than at Harborough Rocks. All sorts of atavistic instincts are roused on a misty morning at the sight of these fantastic outcrops of hardened dolemitic limestone rising steeply from the bare plateau above the High Peak Trail. For a moment one could imagine that on top of this bastion of rock dwells some forgotten race of people like those who inhabited Sir Arthur Conan Doyle's 'Lost World' or James Hilton's 'Shangri-La'.

This vague, fleeting impression is not all that fanciful. Man did inhabit Harborough Cave for several thousand years and the dead were buried in barrows above. And not only man lived in the cave. Before him it was the habitat of numerous animals, as were all the limestone caves of the Peak. Excavations in the accumulations of clay and rubble in various caves have revealed the bones of such animals as the hyena and sabre-toothed tiger that must have roamed the hills when the climate was much wilder than it is today. Other animals: bison, brown bear, Irish elk, lynx, reindeer and wolf must date from the close of the Great Ice Age.

The wolf survived much longer. As late as 1324, the aptly named John de Wolfhunt shared with Thomas Foljambe one bovate of land (about fifteen acres) at Wormhill in return 'for the taking of wolves' from the Peak Forest. It was said that:

> Each year, viz in March and September they ought to go through the middle of the forest and take the wolves in the places they frequented, because in those times the wolves are

not able to smell the dug land as well as at other times of the year. They also went into the forest in dry summers at the feast of St Barnabas when the wolves have whelps to take and destroy them and at no other times; they had with them a servant to carry the traps, and all were sworn and carried a hatchet and a lance with a cutlass or hunting knife attached to their girdles, but neither bow nor arrows. And they had with them a mastiff not lawed, and trained to this work.

The last wolf in the Peak—perhaps the last in England—is said to have been killed early in the fifteenth century, though in Sherwood Forest, not far to the east, a man was appointed 'to frighten away wolves' as late as 1433, and packs survived in Scotland and Ireland until well into the eighteenth century. The memory of this creature is preserved by such Peakland placenames as Wolfscote Dale, Wolfhope and Woolow, a corruption of Wolf Low. Similarly, the wild boar, which was exterminated around the same time as the wolf, has given its name to the village of Wildboarclough.

If these particular creatures have disappeared from the hills and dales, the Peak can still spring its surprises. Over the last thirty years or so, motorists driving at night along roads near the grotesquely shaped gritstone outcrop called The Roaches, on Axe Edge, have occasionally picked out in their headlights the sight of wallabies leaping across the road in front of them, a sight surely as effective as the breathalyser test as a deterrent to mixing drinking with driving. These marsupials are not, of course, survivors from some warmer period in the Peak's history. Like the mink which are occasionally seen round Ladybower, they are escapers from a private collection—the wallabies, but not the mink, from Swythamley Hall. By the end of World War II, there were thought to be over forty of these creatures roaming the district, but the severe winters of 1947 and 1963 reduced the numbers and there are now probably fewer than twenty. At least two sightings were reported in 1974. In May of that year a party of Venture Scouts from Leicestershire encountered three wallabies in broad daylight, and though these young men had not previously heard that marsupials were abroad in the area they were sufficiently alert to take photographs to prove their veracity and their ability to live up to the Scout's motto.

But even without such exotic intruders, and discounting the interesting collection of European animals and birds in the fauna reserve which is open throughout the year to visitors at Riber Castle, near Matlock, the natural history of the Peak is exciting. This is because of its geographical location. As a transitional area—the first or last bastion of Highland Britain —the Peak District marks the northern or southern limit of various species of fauna and flora.

W. H. Hudson made this point more than fifty years ago. After a winter spent in dreaming of seeing exotic birds in far away places, he found himself in the following summer with neither the money nor the leisure to achieve his ambition. So he compromised.

> The longer journey had to be postponed to another year and a shorter one taken; so it came about that I got no further than the Peak district, just to spend a few weeks during the breeding season with half a dozen birds, all familar enough to most ornithologists, but which are not found, at all events not all together, nearer to London than the Derbyshire hills.

He went to Axe Edge 'on the gritstone formation, harsh and desolate in aspect, but covered with a dense growth of heather, bilberry, and coarse grasses—a habitation of birds'. There he found what he sought—'the bird life peculiar to the district —grouse, curlew, golden plover, snipe and summer snipe, water and ring-ousel'.

'On the gritstone formation', you notice. Where birds are concerned, the division between highland and lowland Britain just about coincides with the boundary between the Dark Peak and the White Peak. The bird life on the limestone, except on the barer uplands, is rich in variety, but mainly with species that you are equally likely to see south of the Trent. The gritstone country has far less variety, but much greater distinction. Some species overlap the two areas. Ring ouzels breed in small numbers on the gritstone edges of the High Peak and also on the limestone further south. Water ouzels, or dippers, may be seen near swift-flowing streams on both limestone and gritstone, though infrequently, there being no more than 200 pairs in the whole of the Peak. The little owl was first seen in Derbyshire in 1843, only two years after its introduction into Britain by the eccentric Squire Waterton at Walton Park in Yorkshire, but it was not until the first decade of the twentieth century that it established itself in the county, and then in the south. By the end of World War I it had worked its way north on to the limestone and is now equally at home on the gritstone. The nuthatch is another bird that seems to be working its way northward. But as a generalisation, the distinction is valid. It stems, like most features of the Peak, from those 'stones', and from the different kinds of vegetation that cover the different kinds of soil.

So it is up on the moorland of 'heather, bilberry and coarse bog grasses' that you can hear, as Hudson did, the plaintive cry of the curlew, the 'peep-eep' of the golden plover and the characteristic rasping 'go back, back, back' of the red grouse protecting its territory. These are the traditional birds of the high moorlands, though the meadow pipit is probably more numerous than any other species. A recent survey has revealed that the twite, one of the least common of the finch family, is far more widespread in the Peak than had been suspected. But the red grouse has had more effect on the history and appearance of the gritstone moors than any other bird. The only bird that winters out on the hilltops, it attracted Victorian sportsmen whose gamekeepers guarded the moorland as though it were sacred ground. Sheep and ramblers were kept at bay, while heather and bilberry were encouraged as alternative, less favoured, forms of nutriment. Young heather of around five or six years' growth is the staple diet, and since the red grouse—actually brown with black wings—is a lazy feeder who likes his food near to home, the heather is usually kept close cropped. For nesting, longer heather of around twelve years is preferred, which partly accounts for the patchy appearance of the moors.

Black grouse also breed in small numbers and there have been sightings of the cocks performing their strange courtship dances known as 'leks'. The dunlin nest in small numbers in the cotton-sedge on the highest, soggiest peat moors. Ravens, once fairly widespread in the Peak as several placenames testify, are now rare. The pair that bred on the high moorland in 1966 were the first to do so for over a century and, so far, the last.

The raven must have been driven away from the area during the heyday of game preservation in the second half of the nineteenth century when, to quote Brian Vesey-Fitz-gerald, gamekeepers waged 'incessant war upon predators of all sorts and, indeed, upon any creature which might, just conceivably, prey upon game'. The raven fell into this latter class, and so, as Eric Parker put it, was to be 'put out of a world which should only fitly contain partridges, pheasants, hares, rabbits and gamekeepers', and, of course, grouse, which Parker, a southerner, forgot. Sparrowhawks suffered similar harassment, and were equally unpopular with farmers and shepherds, which is one reason why they were the only predators left out of the Wild Birds Protection Act, 1954, though they were subsequently added to the list. But sparrowhawks survived in small numbers and may still be found on the slopes of such valleys as Longdendale, Woodlands and Edale as well as in the more remote cloughs, which are also the habitat of merlin. These, and the fairly common kestrel, are among the few remaining predators. The short-eared owl, a diurnal species, breeds occasionally but the success of the breeding depends on the number of voles present, which also fluctuates. The only pair of golden eagles known to have nested in the Peak did so more than 250 years ago and have never since attempted so southerly a home.

Some twenty-five years ago, W. H. Pearsall estimated the bird population of a typical upland moor at about 20–50 birds per 100 acres, and this is probably about right for the gritstone area in summer today, though in winter the red grouse are usually left in sole possession of the higher ground. In the remains of the gritstone woodland the population figure must be much higher, though no thorough survey has been carried out. The reservoirs, on the other hand, have attracted a disappointingly small number of aquatic birds, largely because of the depth of the water and lack of shallows, and the absence of suitable shore vegetation. The moorhen breeds in them, the mallard and teal are fairly frequent visitors, the tufted duck arrive in small numbers, while the gannet and even the osprey are occasionally seen on the waters.

If, however, the ornithologist heads for the Dark Peak, as Hudson did, the botanist may find more for his enjoyment on the White Peak. Not that the gritstone moors lack interest. Up there will be found the most southerly habitat of the cloud-berry, flourishing above 1,500ft, especially where the peat has eroded. In places, however, erosion has almost entirely denuded the vegetation, and there has been some plant loss over the last half century owing to pollution spreading across from the industrial areas of north Cheshire and south Lanca-shire, as well as from the lime kilns and quarries close at hand. Significantly, the East Moors, virtually free from industrial pollution since Sheffield has become almost smoke-less, have now the richest flora on the Dark Peak. But farther north in the High Peak there has been an additional reason for a reduction in the number of lichens and the almost total disappearance of Sphagnum moss. This is burning, originally for sheep-grazing, and later, more systematically, for grouse-moor management. As a result the heather has benefited, as has the cotton grass—actually a sedge, *Eriophorum vaginatum* —which replaces the heather and overlies the peat at about 1,500ft.

But, as I say, the average botanist may be happier on the limestone, not only in the dales but also on the many disused industrial sites. One redeeming feature of a limestone quarry is that when men finish extracting its stone a most exciting flora quickly helps to fill the hole that is left behind. Orchids flourish particularly well in such settings. In 1971, admittedly an exceptionally good year, more than 300 flower spikes of the bee orchid were found in one disused quarry in the area between Wirksworth and Middleton, and only a few less in another nearby.

Lead mine spoil-heaps are sometimes equally productive. Some three centuries ago, the great naturalist John Ray remarked on the mountain sandwort, *Minuartia verna,* 'growing on the barren earth they dig out of the shafts of the lead mines near Wirksworth', and it can still be found there in the most southerly area in which it grows in Britain. It seems to flourish, often surrounded only by sheep's fescue, on spoil-heaps where the lead ore content is fairly high. Where the ore is less prevalent the mounds are made more colourful by blue and yellow mountain pansies, purple thyme, blue germander speedwell and, most remarkable of all, the Alpine pennycress, *Thlaspi alpestre,* which grows only in Derbyshire—especially around Matlock—and nowhere else on the mainland of Great Britain. The spoil-heaps of silica sand-pits are apt to display small quantities of the various species of clubmoss which elsewhere in the Peak are now rare.

Unfortunately for naturalists, many of these sites are being reworked in the search for fluorspar and other minerals. In the late 1960s bulldozing on Longstone Edge threatened the

Page 85 The shale valley of the Derwent viewed from the gritstone escarpment of Froggatt Edge

Page 86 (above) Mam Tor, the 'shivering mountain' near Castleton, another 'wonder of the Peak'; *(below)* Hurt's Wood, Dovedale, one of the few remaining survivals of ancient natural woodland in the Peak

rare dark-red helleborine, *Epipactis atrorubens,* first recorded about 1900. Laporte Industries, the largest fluorspar extractors in the Peak, readily accepted a suggestion that a small area where the best plants grew should be fenced off and left unmolested. When a further area was in danger a few years later, members of the Derbyshire Naturalists' Trust, having received early warning of the new threat, transferred 41 plants to a second enclosure close to the first. The transplants seem to have been highly successful.

Of several similar rescue operations, one of the most notable took place a week before Christmas in 1971, when some Trust members transferred a colony of Alpine clubmoss from silica sand-pits that were about to be reworked near Friden to a similar site nearby that already supported colonies of fir clubmoss and stag's-horn moss. This new site has now become a small nature reserve in which these increasingly rare acid-loving plants are preserved. Earlier in the same year, 37 bee orchid plants with flower spikes had been rescued in the nick of time from a sand-pit near Brassington that was being adapted as a reservoir for slurry from the Hopton washing plant, though it was too late to save other plants on the pit floor. A previous attempt to save colonies of bee orchids and fly orchids from the nearby Fallgate Quarry was unsuccessful, the plants being apparently sunk without trace in a sea of slurry. But there is a happier ending to the story of Crich Quarry, where there might have been a clash of conservationists. When the Tramway Museum Society, who occupy the quarry, proposed to extend their car park in 1970 a large colony of bee orchids was threatened by the bulldozer. However, after a meeting with members of the Matlock Field Club, a happy compromise was willingly reached, the Tramway Society agreeing to leave undisturbed the area most thickly populated by orchids, and to delay operations while the rest were transplanted, an exercise that was successfully carried out.

Though limestone quarrying and fluorspar working present the greatest threat to the rich plant life of the Peak, there are dangers from other quarters. Air pollution is one already mentioned, though this is a problem that may be becoming less acute. Sheep, or their absence, may impoverish plant life while encouraging the growth of trees. Enclosures in the half century after 1770, and improvement in methods of agriculture, tended to draw the sheep away from the steep dale sides into flatter fields between the stone walls on the limestone plateau. Freed from the nibbling of sheep, the dalesides began to develop a cover of woodland, shrub and thick masses of grass to the impoverishment of plant life. The pace of this development increased after myxomatosis drastically reduced the rabbit population. For proof of this, one only has to look at seventeenth- and eighteenth-century paintings of Dovedale and other picturesque dales. Invariably, the walls of the dales are shown as rocky and almost treeless. One has to allow for artistic licence. In an age of romance, art patrons liked their landscapes to be suitably craggy and bare, but not all the artists could have been fooling all their patrons all the time.

But above all, the plant life of the Peak is threatened by the most reckless, feckless of all predators: man. Some of the damage he causes is quite involuntary. One pair of human feet will do little damage; half a million pairs will have a devastating effect. But how do you stop people visiting a beautiful spot in increasing numbers? And who would want to stop them anyway? This problem is fortunately confined to only a few places in the Peak. The picking of wild flowers is more common. There seems to be a different standard of morality about taking flowers from taking other property. Cowslips, primroses and lilies of the valley seem to be regarded as anyone's for the picking, and their numbers are obviously declining. The splendid rhododendron gardens at Lea Hall appear to be regarded as fair game by acquisitive visitors. A new threat to the many interesting, and in some instances, rare Peakland mosses is the professional florist and market gardener: a rolling stone who gathers too much moss. But the greatest danger to plant life comes from the thoughtless amateur gardener, or flower lover, who just happens to like some rare plant and thinks that to take just one specimen would do no harm. R. H. Appleby, Chairman of the Derbyshire Naturalists' Trust, tells an amusing story in the September, 1970, *Newsletter* of the Trust, that illustrates this point. A lady was seen in Lathkill Dale carrying a bunch of flowers among which were several maiden pinks. When she was gently told that this was one of Derbyshire's rarities, that the site from which she had just picked them was one of only eight in the county, her companion said, 'Oh, in that case I'd better go back and get some myself.' By the next year the small colony had disappeared.

It is to protect the environment from these and other dangers that nature reserves are established. The Derbyshire Naturalists' Trust, formed in 1961, comparatively late in the post-war, television-led wave of enthusiasm for natural history, now owns, or manages, more than twenty nature reserves in the Peak—varying in size from little more than 1 acre up to more than 60 acres, and amounting in all to more than 350 acres—and there are other reserves administered by various other bodies.

These reserves include a good cross-section of the Peakland flora. The Overdale Reserve, for instance, comprises $44\frac{1}{2}$ acres of upland pasture on shale near Brough. It is neatly divided into three very different parts by two streams flowing northward. At the west end is an area of level grassland, grazed by sheep and cattle which keep the grass under control. A central steep-sided valley contains a stream with a 10ft waterfall on its course. Bracken covers the west side of the valley, but a rich flora beneath the bracken includes numerous woodland species, such as wood sorrel. Heather and crowberry grow on the acid eastern slope of this valley. The stream, besides attracting the ring ouzel, contains some of the most interesting plants in the reserve, such as bog pimpernel and common butterwort. The east side of the reserve is a more open valley on which cotton grass grows, as do the marsh violet and marsh pennywort.

The Deep Dale reserve, Kingsterndale, where the Trust manages 60 acres with the co-operation of four farmers, makes a good contrast, being basically on grassland which is lightly grazed, with some outcropping limestone and scree. The flora, typical of limestone areas, includes harebell, crosswort, purging flax, as well as the familiar cowslip and thyme, but there are some less common plants, including early purple orchid which, with the cowslip, makes a charming spectacle in spring, frog orchid, twayblade, mountain pansy and the lovely late summer grass of Parnassus, a plant which favours the damper, shadier north-facing dale slopes.

It is tantalising, after holding out the promise of such riches, to say that these reserves are, officially, open only to members of the Trust, but the rule is obviously a sensible one. These reserves are reservoirs of wild life, and reservoirs can all too easily be polluted. They are also, to change the metaphor, living laboratories in which the scientist needs to work at his research in solitude with no risk of his specimens being disturbed. But the public is not entirely excluded from all nature reserves. There are four that he will pass through on the Tissington Trail and four more on the High Peak Trail, amounting to around 50 acres in all, that will give him a taste of delight. Railway tracks were in effect nature reserves before anyone thought of the name. Those on the Tissington Trail are especially rich in wild flowers and herbs, particularly at the southern end, and in bird life. The ornithologist may see along the trail black-cap, chiff-chaff, wren, song thrush, meadow pipit, mistle thrush, yellow hammer, and perhaps even the occasional kestrel, redstart or wheatear.

NATURAL HISTORY

To the most important nature reserve in Peakland, there is no access. This is the 158 acre Derbyshire Dales National Nature Reserve that was established in 1972 by the Nature Conservancy as the first national reserve in the Peak. It is in two parts. In Lathkill Dale are 123 acres of ash and elm woodland. Some five miles or so to the north-west, as the ring ouzel flies, in Monks Dale are 35 acres of limestone outcrop and screes, scrub and grassland. Between them they offer, it has been said, 'some of the best examples of woodland, grassland and scrub on carboniferous limestone in Britain'.

Beneath the canopy of trees in the Lathkill Dale reserves, the astonishingly rich variety of shrubs includes mezereon whose fragrant pink flowers are rarely seen now in early spring in the calcareous woods of the south, owing to the acquisitiveness of local gardeners, and only in the Peak in about half a dozen sites. The flowering plants are equally varied, but very different from those of Monk's Dale, which include that rare Derbyshire native the spring cinquefoil, *Potentilla tabernaemontani*, the Nottingham catchfly, which flourishes more widely on south-facing limestone slopes in Derbyshire than anywhere else in Britain and the rarish herb paris, a strange plant whose single greenish flower surmounts a whorl of four leaves.

Although grazing and the demands of the lead-mining industry have changed the face of most of these woodlands over the centuries, a few remnants of ancient natural woodland survive, usually on the less-accessible dale sides, as in Monk's Dale, Cressbrook Dale and Hurt's Wood in Dovedale, amongst the boulders on the steep slopes of the gritstone cloughs and below the edges. Padley Wood, between the Derwent and the gritstone escarpment, has been carefully studied by C. D. Pigott. In medieval times, before clearance and grazing, it was an extensive oak wood. Because the ground was too rough and rocky for regular grazing, portions have survived as mixed oak and birch wood with occasional rowan, and extensive alder on the damper lower slopes. But the sheep that wander into the area prevent the extensive regeneration of the oaks, nearly half of which are between 100 and 300 years old, and the birches, which regenerate freely, are gradually becoming the predominant trees. In the shade of the trees, the large heaps of twigs and leaf midribs cover the nests of the northern type of wood ant, *Formica rufa,* which is not found further to the south-east.

The newer coniferous woodlands have little ground vegetation and therefore support few ground insects apart from a small number of moths whose larvae feed on pine needles, but a more varied selection of moths is found on the high moorland where their larvae feed on heather or bilberry. The limestone dales are vastly richer in insects, including the glow-worm, which was thought to be extinct thereabouts until seven larvae were seen—'each glowing like a small piece of silver paper'—in Hopton Quarry in 1969. Since then others have been observed and at the time of writing the Derbyshire Naturalists' Trust is carrying out a glow-worm survey.

The butterfly population in the Peak, as elsewhere, has declined over the last century, but there are heartening signs that some species have returned to the dales in the last few years. The dark green fritillary has re-established itself since 1937 in a few dales, and its close relative, the small pearl-bordered fritillary, was seen in the Via Gellia in 1970 and again in 1971, 70 years after its previous recording. The peacock butterfly, after several years when it failed to appear, became widespread and common in 1969. After this boom year its numbers again declined, but it is still fairly common in the Matlock area. Close by, at Cromford, the white letter hairstreak was discovered on wych elm in 1970 and it now seems that the species has returned to this part of the Derwent Valley after several years' absence.

Of the mammal population, the resident most likely to

interest the visiting naturalist is the mountain, or blue hare, one of the few creatures that inhabit the deep acid blanket peat of the High Peak. Native to the area in prehistoric times, as bones in caves have revealed, it died out, probably around 4000 BC, and was re-introduced to the Peak from the Scottish Highlands about 1870–80. It feeds on heather and cotton grass between 900ft and 1,800ft, has no predators to fear beyond an occasional buzzard and after a series of mild winters, it is at least maintaining its population. In summer it is easily distinguishable from its close relative the brown hare, also common in the Peak, though it is slightly smaller and stockier and its fur has a slightly grey-blue tinge that accounts for its name. But in mid-winter the fur turns almost completely white and remains so until early April, a piece of anti-predator camouflage which has in fact made it more conspicuous during a series of comparatively snowless winters.

The stoat, which in the Peak is less common than the weasel, especially since the decline of the rabbit population, only adopts a white coat—and then only partially—in exceptionally hard winters.

The red squirrel population is declining in the Peak, as in other parts of Britain, in the face of the advance of the grey squirrel, but a few reds may still be found in coniferous woodlands. Badgers are fairly common, despite illegal badger digging, and their tracks can be seen across the Tissington and High Peak Trails, among other places.

Visitors to Chatsworth will almost certainly be rewarded by a distant view of fallow deer, and there is another herd in Stanton Park. A herd of red deer have inhabited Lyme Park since 1300. South Derbyshire seems to be the northern limit of the muntjak, but there has been one recent sighting at Fenny Bentley at the extreme southern limit of the national park.

Otters are unhappily rare in the Peak, which may be one reason why, by way of compensation, the crawfish survives in the fast-flowing limestone rivers, where it hides under stones and in holes in the bank by day, emerging at night to feed on insect larvae and snails which it grabs with long pincers. This lobster-like creature, known locally as 'crawkie', is the largest invertebrate found in fresh water, growing to 4in long.

The limestone rivers of the Peak are chiefly famed for their trout fishing. One immediately thinks of the Dove, Wye and Lathkill as the home of the brown trout, but trout also inhabit the Derwent reservoirs, that river itself below the reservoirs and indeed almost all the Peakland streams, which are amongst the cleanest waters in Britain. The lower Amber alone is affected by industrial pollution from the east and this is not sufficient to prevent coarse fishing in the Derwent below the confluence at Ambergate. The American rainbow trout which was probably introduced into some Derbyshire rivers around the time that the weirs were constructed on the Dove sometime in the first half of the nineteenth century, now breeds naturally in the Wye and in no other English river, according to the local experts. By the riverside walk near Bakewell Bridge they virtually queue up to receive tit-bits thrown into the water by picnickers. Grayling, Charles Cotton's 'dead-hearted fish', seem to avoid both the head-waters and lower reaches of rivers, inhabiting the Derwent mainly between Bamford Weir and Cromford, the Wye and its main tributaries and the Dove and Manifold. Angling in Derbyshire is a joy to those armed with the necessary licence from the Severn–Trent Water Authority and the consent of the riparian owner or tenant, but in some areas fishing rights are strictly private.

6   THE RIVERS

TALK of fish in Peakland rivers leads almost instinctively to the Dove and to recollections of Izaak Walton and Charles Cotton, the piscator and the viator of the second part of *The Compleat Angler*. They were an oddly contrasted couple; the gentle, pious 'father of angling' and the hard drinking, gambling squire of Beresford Hall, but they were united by one shared enthusiasm—angling—and on the Dove they were able to enjoy to the full their chosen sport.

Three hundred years have passed since the initials of Walton and Cotton were intwined above the door of the grey limestone fishing house under the legend *Piscatoribus sacrum,* 1674, but in that time little has changed along the Dove, except that vegetation is more luxuriant and that Cotton's old home is now a ruin. The fishing house stands intact, though unfortunately on private land. I say 'unfortunately', from the tourists' viewpoint, but perhaps it is as well. It might otherwise be in danger from vandals, as indeed it was early in the nineteenth century. A visitor in 1814 described it as 'much dilapidated, the windows unglazed, and the wainscot and pavement gone'. Later in the century it was carefully restored and it remains in good condition.

Further downstream the little packhorse bridge at Milldale is now scheduled as an ancient monument. This is Viator's Bridge, which drew from Walton the comment, 'What's here? Do you use to travel in wheelbarrows in this country? This bridge certainly was made for nothing else. Why a mouse can hardly go over it; it is but two fingers broad!'

It is sufficiently wide to carry something like half a million walkers a year, but farther downstream still is a much wider bridge that Walton probably never knew and now hardly carries any traffic at all. This is Coldwell Bridge at Thorpe, beyond the famous stepping-stones and rarely visited by tourists. Indeed one's first impression is that it was built for no other purpose than the sheer pleasure of bridge building. But a milestone at its east end incribed 'Cheadle 11 miles', and faint indications in the grass on either side make it clear that this bridge, more than a hundred yards long, once carried the important coach road between Ashbourne and Cheadle over the Dove. The '1726' incribed on this now grass-covered bridge may date its widening rather than its original building.

Beyond Thorpe, which is a charming limestone village with a prominent squat Norman church tower, the valley widens and loses some of the dramatic quality as it bubbles southward to join the Trent in south-west Derbyshire, but even after it has left the Peak far behind and becomes a river of the Midland Plain it retains a great deal of charm. Of all its 45 miles there is not one that can be called dull. But we must leave it at Coldwell Bridge, echoing Izaak Walton's farewell: 'Well, go thy way, little Dove! thou art the finest river that ever I saw and the fullest of fish.'

Byron was equally moved to ecstasy by the Dove. 'Was you ever in Dovedale?' he once wrote to the Irish poet Tom Moore, who in fact lived for a time by the Dove at Mayfield. 'I assure you', Byron continued, 'there are things in Derbyshire as noble as in Greece or Switzerland.' And he might have found almost equal nobility in Staffordshire if he had crossed the Dove to look at its tributary the Manifold. But the Manifold has always tended to receive less publicity than its neighbour, partly because it is even less accessible. Except between 1904 and 1934, when it could be reached by railway from Leek, the valley has always been virtually ignored by public transport. Today private transport is the only effective way of reaching all but the lowest reach of the Manifold, but the motor car is much less useful for exploring the valley because the river—even when it is not running underground—is often out of sight of any motor road. Pressure by motoring organisations for the track of the disused Leek and Manifold Light Railway to be opened as a motor road throughout its entire length have been, rightly, resisted. The track—apart from a short section open to light vehicles between Redhurst Halt and Butterton Station—remains a pleasant footpath, as it has been since the Staffordshire County Council accepted it as a gift from the Light Railway Company in 1937 and set a most welcome precedent in finding this use for abandoned railways.

The comparative inaccessibility adds immeasurably to the charm of the Manifold. It is a river for the angler in search of trout and grayling, and for the walker. But the motor car is not wholly a white elephant in the Manifold country; it has its uses. I have explored the valley fully on foot, but I have also used a combination of car and feet. That way you get the best of two worlds; the intimate exploration of a valley that is little inferior to the Dove in its mixture of ruggedness and charm combined with the exhilaration—rare in modern England—of dramatic drives down twisting narrow roads that plunge steeply into deep valleys and then climb equally steeply and crookedly up the other side.

One such road descends from the 1,000ft limestone plateau at Wetton to the river at Weag's Bridge, 650ft below. A short distance beyond Wetton one of several hairpin bends offers a dramatic view of Thor's Cave, lofty and spacious, whose interior has revealed traces of human occupation during every period between Mesolithic and Roman times. From Weag's Bridge the road winds around another blind, narrow corner to rise just as steeply to regain the plateau on the other side of the river at Grindon, a scattered village with a wide

97

common—a rarity in the Peak—and a Victorian church.

Beyond the village, from Grindon Moor, there are superb views of green conical hills—Ecton Hill, Manor House and Sheen Hill among them, rising to around 1,200ft—that separate the valleys of Manifold and Dove. Then the road falls steeply to cross the Hoo Brook, a tributary of the Manifold, by a deep ford. In fact for some thirty yards the bed of the brook is the road, running between stone walls so that one has the feeling of entering some tiny Cornish fishing harbour by boat. Then dry ground is regained, and the road climbs again to Butterton village before descending once more to the river at Swainsley.

A car is also decidedly useful for exploring the upper reaches of the river. It rises on Axe Edge, 1,700ft above sea level, within sight of the Buxton–Leek road. There, if you can lower your eyes from the distant view of the Wrekin, forty miles or so to the south-west, you will see the infant Manifold oozing out of a swamp a few hundred yards east of the road.

But after the first headlong descent of 700ft in 1½ miles, the river has little to offer for its next few miles as it cuts deeply into limestone and shales. The valley widens and the river runs through quiet grazing country past Longnor and Brund Mill, though this quietness is periodically threatened by suggestions that yet another reservoir may be built hereabouts.

Where the river enters the limestone just below Hulme End, the scene changes dramatically. The river twists and turns like a snake through its deep, narrow gorge, supporting the theory that its name simply means 'many folds'. Hulme End was the terminus of the light railway, and its station buildings and engine shed now house road-maintenance equipment. Elsewhere the station buildings have gone, though the bridges and Swainsley Tunnel remain.

That the line should ever have been built seems incredible,

for, as is said locally, 'it started from nowhere and finished in the same place'. The promoters, who built 8 miles of narrow gauge track along the valleys of the Manifold and Hamps to join—at Waterhouses—the North Staffordshire Company's standard gauge branch line to Leek, 10 miles farther on, hoped to catch not only the increasing milk trade from the local farms and the growing tourist traffic, but also to encourage a revival of lead and copper mining round Ecton. But they were unlucky. In its 30 years of active life the line provided enjoyment for tourists but not a single dividend for its unfortunate shareholders.

The Ecton copper mines, which had closed about 1890, did not reopen. Their heyday had been a century earlier, when their annual output of 12 tons was four times the total from all the Cornish mines. About that time, when convoys of packhorses left the mines daily to cross the moors to the smelting works at Whiston in the Churnet Valley, John Byng, visiting the mines, was 'stunned' by the noise of the pumping engine, and a little shocked at the sight of 'the many children employ'd in the laborious pounding of the stone, by which hard work they *may* gain 6d per day'.

Ecton today is rather a forlorn place, a sort of industrial Stonehenge, where industrial archaeologists are offered a bewildering array of disused buildings, mine shafts and adit channels, and the sites of a cheese factory and a button factory.

It is a couple of miles or so beyond Ecton, below Redhurst Cliff, that the river goes underground, despite the efforts of enterprising locals in the 1830s to stop up the fissures in the limestone bed. And in all but the wettest weather it remains underground through perhaps the loveliest, and certainly the most thickly wooded, part of the valley, past the isolated ruins of Throwley Old Hall, which Sampson Meverell rebuilt in 1603, until it reappears in the grounds of Ilam Hall, less than a mile from its confluence with the Dove. Dr Johnson, always stubbornly sceptical of natural phenomena, refused to believe that the Manifold was in part a subterranean river even when he was told that corks put into the water near Wetton Mill had in due course reappeared in the river at Ilam.

The Manifold is wholly a Staffordshire river; the Dove for most of its course has one bank in either county, but the Derwent belongs entirely to Derbyshire and indeed, as Camden noted some four centuries ago, it divides the county into two parts from north to south, though it runs fairly close to the eastern edge of the Peak. As well as being the area's chief river it is its most underrated. Hardly anyone has sung its praises loudly, and before Walt Unsworth's *Portrait of the River Derwent* appeared in 1971 nobody had ever written a book about it. This may be an instance of familiarity breeding contempt because, unlike the Dove and Manifold, it is a very public river in the sense that after it runs down from the gritstone it is almost always visible from some main road. On the other hand, it is not an approachable river in that—again unlike the Dove and Manifold—it lacks a public footpath running along its banks, except in short stretches. So, while many people know the Derwent slightly, few know it well. This is a pity because it is an interesting river and in parts a beautiful one.

Defoe called it 'a fury of a river . . . a frightful creature when the hills load her current with water', a judgement that would still be accepted in Matlock, where one inhabitant told me, 'we've 'ad as many floods as we've 'ad 'ot dinners'. But in other places along its banks various flood prevention schemes have at least reduced the risks. Indeed, the Derwent has been messed about a good deal by man; especially by the former Derwent Valley Water Board engineers who controlled its flow from their reservoirs, by various mill owners who used it to supply them with power, and by Capability Brown who, in the 1760s, straightened its course through Chatsworth Park to prevent flooding—or at least to pass the flood waters on to other riparian landowners farther downstream—and to provide a more romantic view from the windows of Chatsworth, where, earlier in the century, James Paine had built a balustraded bridge that remains the most beautiful bridge of its kind in the Peak.

Indeed the hand of man has not marred or polluted the river, in its upper and middle reaches anyway, and many of his bridges at least stand comparison with Paine's masterpiece. There is a delightful humpbacked one at Baslow that was mentioned in a decree of 1500 that 'no one shall henceforth lead or carry any millstone over the bridge of Basselowe under pain of 6/8d', and it was no doubt to prevent such practices that the little guard-post—not much taller than a dog-kennel now, probably because of alterations in the road level—was erected. Not much larger was the fifteenth-century chapel on Cromford Bridge. This bridge-chapel—one of the six that survive in England—was despoiled at the Reformation but partly restored in the 1940s by the Derbyshire Archaeological Society. Close by is an eighteenth-century fishing house with a pyramidal roof and the same inscription, *Piscatoribus sacrum*, as the more famous one in Beresford Dale. An inscription on the parapet of the bridge records 'The leap of R.M.B.H. Mare. June. 1697'. It commemorates the escape of one Benjamin Haywood, whose horse took fright and leaped at least fifteen feet over the parapet and into the river before wading ashore with both horse and rider unharmed. Cromford, Matlock and Whatstandwell bridges all date from around the fifteenth century and all have been subsequently widened. The two latter are not popular with motorists, who have to negotiate bends of almost ninety degrees at each end of both bridges. They must be happier that Baslow Bridge has been bypassed and that a wider modern bridge, opened in 1974, now runs alongside the narrower eighteenth-century structure at Calver under the shadow of a splendidly solid textile mill.

But there is more to the Derwent than its bridges. It is a

lovely river, wild in its upper reaches, but nowhere more beautiful than in Chatsworth Park and southwards to Ambergate, sharing for much of the way below Matlock its narrow valley floor with road, railway and the Cromford Canal.

On its way it receives several atractive tributaries. The first important one is the Noe, which rises above Upper Booth, where it takes in the Crowden Brook and then flows on by Barber Booth into the Vale of Edale. Hemmed in by massive hills on either side it is forced north-westward until it finds a passage between Lose Hill and Win Hill and is able to turn due south into the wider Vale of Hope. As a river of the gritstone and shales it may lack something of the sparkling freshness of the limestone streams and the lush vegetation of their banks, but its surroundings are superb. The best way to see the Noe is to follow the ridge along the whaleback of Rushup Edge, passing the hill fort on Mam Tor's summit and on by Lose Hill, hardly dropping below 1,500ft along the way until you descend into the valley just north of Hope. From the ridge there are magnificent views of the Kinder massif above Edale on the one hand and along the green, fertile Hope valley on the other. The only jarring note in the Hope Valley is struck by the smoke rising from the tall chimney of the cement works at Bradwell. But in fairness, it must be said that the works was there long before the National Park existed, that it is vital to the local economy and that after much prodding by local conservationists, followed after 1951 by the Peak Park Planning Board, the works' management has become acutely conscious of the need to protect the valley's beauty. The result of all this has been some most effective landscaping. But it is difficult to landscape a pall of smoke.

Swollen by the addition of Peakshole Water, which joins it south of Hope church, and the Bradwell Brook that flows in at Brough, the Noe is quite a sizable river when it reaches its confluence with the Derwent at Bamford despite the fact

Page 103 (above) Arbor Low, Peakland's most impressive prehistoric monument; (below) Peveril Castle, Castleton, the twelfth-century keep

Page 104 (left) Winster Market Hall, a National Trust property; *(right)* Woodhead Tunnel. The building of the two disused tunnels on the left cost

that water from all three streams has been extracted and fed by tunnels under the hills into Ladybower reservoir. The poaching of water from these streams was an afterthought to the original Derwent Valley scheme made necessary by an unexpected increase in the thirst of the towns, and the whole operation was not completed until 1960. But even that does not end the story of man's assault on the Derwent and its tributaries. At Bamford, water from the main stream passes through filter beds and is then channelled through underground pipes and aqueducts by gravity flow to a service reservoir at Ambergate, from where branches run east and south.

Fortunately, man's interference with the Derwent has not been so obvious as to spoil it—if you accept the majority opinion that favours the reservoirs. But in places he has laid clumsier hands on its next tributary, the Wye. Quarries south of Buxton scar the banks and leave a film of milky lime on the surface of the water for a mile or two. Where Great Rocks Dale runs off the main valley, gaunt lime-kilns stand up against a backcloth of bare rocks. Further downstream there are textile mills, while the track of the abandoned St Pancras– Manchester railway line—sometimes out of sight in tunnels, sometimes crossing and re-crossing on bridges and viaducts— keeps company with the river for much of its course. All this might have ruined the river irretrievably, as Ruskin feared, but somehow this has not happened. Scars there are, but only a few major blemishes, and these are all left behind after the first four or five miles.

For the most part the Wye is a typically clear and sparkling limestone river, though it rises on the gritstone 1,100ft up on the eastern slopes of Axe Edge. From there it drops as a clear mountain stream into the heart of Buxton, where in places it is tucked away out of sight in culverts and in others it is allowed to run rather self-consciously through public parks and gardens with something of the attitude of a small boy made to wear his best suit and keep out of mischief. And then, on the southern outskirts of the town, it is subject to worse indignities, being confined for a short distance between the A6 trunk road, with all its whirling confusion of traffic, and the disused railway line to Miller's Dale.

Yet even this stretch through Ashwood Dale, so thickly wooded on both banks that branches almost form a canopy overhead, must once have been lovely, and even today offers glimpses of great beauty for those in the passenger seats of a car. But the Wye—like the Manifold—is not really a motorist's river. True, there are places where it runs alongside the A6—as at Ashford-in-the-Water—and there is an unforgettable view from the road at the foot of Taddington Hill, where the river takes a great sweep round Shacklow Wood, so notably enriched in the great programme of planting carried out by the fifth Duke of Rutland and his Duchess Elizabeth in the first quarter of the nineteenth century. (Although the Department of the Environment has tried to make the view forgettable by some unwise road straightening in 1973 against the advice of the Peak Park Planning Board.) But there are many glorious stretches that can be enjoyed only on foot, which is perhaps why they remain glorious. There is luckily no room for a motor road through Chee Dale, or the best parts of Miller's Dale, Cressbrook Dale or Monsal Dale. So the sensible thing to do is drive or use the bus through Ashwood Dale, too good at its best to be ignored, and then explore the rest of the river on foot.

This exploration will reveal that if man has attempted to disfigure the valley with his quarries, he has at least partly redressed the balance with his bridges. Two of the best are in Bakewell. The town bridge, built about 1300, has five Gothic arches facing downstream, and though the upstream side has been modernised, it has been done so tactfully as not to be obstrusive. A little to the north, close to a former cotton mill of Sir Richard Arkwright's, a packhorse bridge links the main

road to the hamlet of Holme and its delightful Jacobean
mansion, Holme Hall, across the meadows. Two miles upstream, Ashford-in-the-Water has, besides an exquisite name
and a small but pleasing tithe barn, three fine bridges. The
most attractive is Sheepwash Bridge at the north end of the
village near the church, where sheep were still washed until
recently under the lee of the bridge.

In the grounds of Haddon Hall are two more charming
bridges. The one over which you approach the house dates
from 1663. The other was reputedly the spot where Dorothy
Vernon, escaping hurriedly on the eve of a loveless marriage,
met her lover John Manners, and eloped with him to their wedding at Aylestone in Leicestershire. No matter if, as the purists
say, the bridge was not built until after Dorothy's elopement
in 1558—if she ever did elope—it certainly looks a perfect
setting for a lover's tryst, and even without its romantic
trappings it is still a fine example, on the small scale, of the
bridge-builder's art.

But more later of Haddon, which represents the romantic
aspect of the Wye, overlooking the wide restful meadows of
the river's lower reaches. Cressbrook Mill, higher up the
valley in an equally romantic setting, displays the river's
workaday face in a surprisingly attractive light. The main
building, dating from 1815, has a noble pediment in the
centre with a lantern surmounting a hipped roof. Facing it,
higher up the slope to the north, is a row of cottages that was
once the apprentice house. At the west end of the block, facing
the river, is a derelict Gothic building that must once have
been the chapel for the apprentices, who were treated at
Cressbrook with more consideration than was usual for that
time.

The mill-owner, William Newton, a self-educated poet and
man-of-letters, and protégé of Anna Seward who hailed him as
'Minstrel of the Peak', saw to it that 'the children's hours of
work and their necessary relaxation are kindly and judiciously

arranged', according to a Mrs Sterndale, who visited the
mill in 1824 and pointed out the contrast with conditions
prevailing in Lancashire and Yorkshire mills. 'Their food',
she wrote, 'is of the best quality and amply dispensed: they
have eight hours' uninterrupted sleep in comfortable beds
and airy rooms.'

She would have found an equally sharp contrast if she had
walked upstream a couple of miles to Litton Mill, through a
beautiful and secluded part of the valley known as Water-cum-
Jolly and now a haunt of budding rock-climbers and of
botanists seeking the rare bird's-foot sedge and the twisted
podded whitlow-grass which flourish hereabouts. At Litton the
apprenticeship system was at its most brutal, according to
one Robert Blincoe, who survived it to write a memorable
account of his appalling experience there. Both mills then
spun cotton, but at the time of writing they are both idle.

Another industry associated with the Wye died about 1905.
This was the quarrying and working of Ashford marble, a
dark grey bituminous marble once very fashionable for fireplaces and ornaments. The marble mill, founded in 1748 by
Henry Watson, son of Samuel Watson who did much of the
ornamental stonework and wood carving at nearby Chatsworth, is still marked on the map (SK 190694), but much of
the site lies under the A6 and the rest is a depot of the Severn–
Trent Water Authority.

About two miles above Ashford, Headstone Head offers
the most spectacular view of the Wye valley. From the car
park there is a magnificent view of the river as it comes down
from the direction of Cressbrook and winds sharply round
the bare slopes of Fin Cop to enter Monsal Dale. Below, is
Monsal Viaduct, which Ruskin had particularly in mind
when he fulminated against those who had carried the railway
through the valley, 'blasted its rocks away, heaped thousands
of tons of shale into its lovely stream. The valley is gone and
the Gods with it, and now every fool in Buxton can be at

Bakewell in half an hour, and every fool in Bakewell in Buxton.'

But Ruskin was wrong. The viaduct, instead of ruining the valley, added something of value: life perhaps, and movement; or perhaps a sense of the littleness of man's efforts against the grand scale of nature. Whatever it was, when the workmen came to take up the track and spoke of demolishing the viaduct the Ruskins of the 1960s wanted it to remain. Eventually the engineers found that the physical problems of demolition and its consequent cost would be prohibitive; so the bridge stays and everyone seems to be happy.

Despite industry and its trappings, then, the Derbyshire Wye remains one of the loveliest short rivers in England, and not far from Haddon Hall it is joined by the combined Lathkill and Bradford, which unite at Alport, about a mile from their confluence with the Wye. Both are unspoilt trout streams; both flow wholly on limestone. The erratic infancy of the Lathkill, I have already described. The Bradford has an almost equally strange birth. It must once have risen near Mouldridge Grange at the southern end of Gratton Dale and been enlarged by a tributary coming in along Long Dale from the west. But both these dales are now dry and you have to walk the two mile length of Gratton Dale to find the present source at Dale End.

As a river the Bradford is short but decidedly sweet. It is a microcosm of all the Peak's limestone rivers. Bradford Dale is only a mile long, but, as J. B. Firth said, 'for peaceful loveliness and sheer prettiness nothing in Derbyshire excels it'. Less pretty is the story of how Fullwood's Rock acquired its name. Sir Christopher Fullwood was a Royalist who enlisted a thousand lead miners in the Civil War. But his house in Middleton-by-Youlgreave was surprised by a Parliamentary force and destroyed. Fullwood escaped into the Dale below and hid between the rock and the rest of the cliff face, where he was soon flushed out and shot, receiving wounds from which he died later. A different kind of shooting went on at Middleton more than three centuries later when part of an episode for the television series, *Country Matters* (based on the short stories of H. E. Bates and A. E. Coppard), was filmed there. Middleton and Alport apart, there are no villages on the Bradford, though Youlgreave sits above it on its long shelf.

The slightly longer Lathkill is even more sparsely populated. Its lovely dale is too narrow for settlement, though Over Haddon bears much the same relationship to it as Youlgreave does to the Bradford, looking down to its dale from an even greater height. Immediately opposite is the charmingly named Meadow Place Grange. A short distance below Over Haddon, the narrow, medieval Conksbury Bridge carries what was once the main highroad from Bakewell to Newhaven Inn and Ashbourne across the Lathkill, though the arches of the bridge are so low that from a distance it looks like a stone wall damming the stream. From a distance, too, the old road seems to descend on either side in a series of alarmingly steep, sharp spirals; but this time there is no illusion. Hereabouts the south side of the river is the National Nature Reserve. A little below the bridge, Raper Lodge made an appearance in the film of D. H. Lawrence's *The Virgin and the Gipsy*, and it would be hard to think of a more perfect setting.

All this may make the Lathkill sound an idyllic river, as Charles Cotton thought when he called it 'by many degrees, the purest and most transparent stream that I ever yet saw, either at home or abroad . . .', and many a widely travelled angler would say the same today. But it would be a mistake to think that man has been content to leave the river untouched. You can see today many signs that the old lead miners were here. And not only lead miners tried to exploit the valley. In 1854 the Lathkill had its Gold Rush. This followed a claim that gold had been found in a bed of toadstone in a disused lead mine; nearly two ounces of fine gold per ton of ore, it was said. Pound shares rose to over £30 as the speculators rushed in. But the gold proved to be iron pyrites—'fools' gold'—and within two years the Over Haddon Gold and Silver Mine was no more than a gleam in the eye of the Official Receiver. Today, with the lead mine traces adding a touch of romance to the scene, the Lathkill really is idyllic.

Two other tributaries of the Derwent, though not quite in the same league as those discussed so far, are worth mentioning. The Amber rises on the gritstone on the south-eastern edge of the East Moors and skirts the western extremity of the Coal Belt before joining the Derwent at Ambergate. On its way, the Amber passes Ashover, a delightful, scattered, up-and-down village that is often missed by visitors to the Peak, Pentrich, famous for its ill-fated, crack-brained but almost noble revolution of 1817, and the quite noble ruins of that splendid, fortified, Wingfield Manor, where Mary, Queen of Scots, was imprisoned for a time. But these two latter places really lie off the Peak, as does much of the other tributary, the Ecclesbourne, which rises near Wirksworth and flows through peaceful, pastoral country dominated by Alport Hill, with the masts of the Derbyshire police radio station on the summit, before joining the Derwent at Duffield among the last foothills of the Pennines just north of Derby.

The three other main rivers of the Peak flow westward to the Irish Sea. Two of them indeed—the Etherow and the Goyt—combine, along with the Tame from farther north, to form the Mersey, an incongruous end to highland streams that begin among the heather on the gritstone moors where the curlews cry, and even the Dane reaches the Mersey eventually after a circuitous route that suggests a natural reluctance to accept this fate.

The Etherow has perhaps the best claim to be the true source of the Mersey because it rises farther to the east than its rivals and follows a reasonably direct westerly course to the sea. Before April 1974 it could be said that the Etherow rose almost at the meeting point of Yorkshire, Derbyshire and Cheshire. For its first 9 miles it was the boundary between the two latter counties. But Cheshire is out of it now, that long narrow tongue of land shooting out along Longdendale having been given to Derbyshire. The source of the Etherow must have been a wild spot a century or more ago when there were a score of hill farms hereabouts and the Pennine shepherds used to meet periodically at the inn at Saltersbrook after rounding up their sheep, but the farms and the sheep were cleared away to allow more space for grouse, and the inn closed. This must temporarily have made the spot even wilder, but today the sense of remoteness is marred by the sound of heavy traffic grinding up the main road through Longdendale. Indeed the Etherow has been tamed to a controlled trickle as it passes through a chain of reservoirs on its way to the cotton mill country in the valley, though it receives tributaries like the Saltersbrook and Crowden Great and Little Brooks that have come down from the wilderness.

In some ways the Goyt has a similar history to the Etherow, in that it now feeds reservoirs and has become a wholly Derbyshire river (by a boundary change in 1928) instead of being shared with Cheshire, but it has somehow managed to retain more of its beauty and charm, surprisingly because though it was described in 1908 as being 'little known to tourists' it is now almost as popular as the Dove. From its source in the peat bogs near the famous Cat and Fiddle Inn it can be followed by a pleasant riverside walk down to Whaley Bridge, 8 miles away, where its attractions lessen. The motorist will find the upper reach much less accessible, though on Sundays in high summer he can use the Peak Park's mini-bus service, which will lead him to some of the more attractive bits, and enable him to see the acres of rhododendrons planted by the Grimshawe family of Errwood Hall and the few remains of this once great Victorian mansion. Peat bogs and rhododendrons may seem strange companions, but then the Goyt Trough is strange country, the result of violent folding and contorting in the gritstone which produces dramatic changes in the scenery and makes the river eminently explorable.

The Dane is equally worth exploring, though its transition from a mountain tarn to a river of the plains is more gradual, most orthodox but hardly less beautiful. This transition from the purple moors to the green of the Cheshire Plain takes place over a distance of about eight miles, during which it is the Staffordshire–Cheshire boundary, Derbyshire having been left behind at Three Shires Head, a much-photographed beauty spot where a single-arched stone bridge crosses Panniers Pool and where, it is said, illegal prize fights and cock fights used to take place. The valley is deep, the scenery wild and rocky and the placenames magnificent. Names like Wincle and Flash convey something of the starkness of the upland villages perched high above the Dane among hills called Cut-thorn, Birchenough, Gradbach, Hawk's Nest and Green Gutter Head. On this magnificently romantic stage, according to R. W. V. Elliott's recent research, an unknown contemporary of Chaucer set much of his famous poem *Sir Gawain and the Green Knight*. The small cave known as Lud's Church, reputedly used by Lollards as a refuge, has been identified as the Green Chapel sought by Sir Gawain; Swythamley Hall, a medieval hunting lodge, as the site of the Green Knight's castle; all the other pieces in this literary jig-saw puzzle seem to fit equally well. And there can be few stretches of wild country in England better fitted to form the background to a medieval romance.

7   COMMUNICATIONS

'ON the roads of Derbyshire travellers were in constant fear for their necks', wrote Macaulay, of England in the reign of James I, 'and were frequently compelled to alight and lead their horses.' Even if we accept the modern belief that Macaulay tended to overstate his case, there is ample evidence that here at least he was not guilty of exaggeration. Edward Browne, who had first-hand experience of the Peak in the mid-seventeenth century, wrote with feeling of 'the craggy ascents, the rocky unevenness of the roads, the high peaks and the almost perpendicular descents'. Only a few years later Celia Fiennes was equally appalled by 'the steepness and hazard of the Wayes—if you take a wrong way there is no passing—you are forced to have Guides in all parts of Darbyshire, and unless it be a few that used to be guides the common people know not above 2 or 3 miles from their home, but they of the country will climb up and down with their horses those steep precipices.'

Three centuries later it is still difficult for the 'common people', unless they have motor cars, to get around in the Peak. Indeed, it is more difficult in the 1970s than it was in the 1870s, when the railway engineers, after many years of frustration, seemed to be overcoming the problems set by the 'steepness and hazard of the Wayes'. The railways came and went again, defeated by 'the almost perpendicular descents' of their profit margins. Bus services tend to be fragmentary, especially in the south-west; except on the fringes and in the valleys, it is a matter of finding out the day rather

than the time of the next bus. Significantly, when the pro-
prietor-driver of the one upland village bus service was
committed to jail in 1973 the villagers petitioned for his
release on the grounds that they had themselves virtually
received a sentence of imprisonment in their own village.

So today one needs a good pair of legs and a motor car—in
that order—to get the most enjoyment out of life in the Peak.
If the hills are no less steep than they were in the seventeenth
century, the roads are now well maintained. One Sheffield
commuter living in remote Offerton told me that so good was
the snow plough service provided by the Derbyshire County
Council that on only one day in the ten winters he had
spent there had the track leading to the tiny hamlet been
impassable.

That track, a narrow, twisting, unfenced way across an open
hillside, and insufficiently dignified to be called a lane, is
probably fairly typical of what most Peakland roads were like
before the mid-eighteenth century. That particular track
may not be prehistoric, but the straighter tracks along the
ridges undoubtedly are. Professor Boyd Dawkins, who knew
the area and its archaeology better than most other people,
believed that the track running from Hope by Mam Tor
and along Rushup Edge had prehistoric origins. R. W. P.
Cockerton has traced the course of the ancient Portway from
extreme south-eastern Derbyshire through Derby, over Harthill Moor to Ashford, Wardlow and on to Edale or Chapel.
Placenames like Ridgeway and Holloway suggest trackways
already well established when the Anglo-Saxon settlers arrived.

It is usually assumed that the Romans were the first people
who made ways—the word 'road' was not used before Tudor
times—but Boyd Dawkins thought that some stretches in
the Peak were laid down in Iron-Age times and later improved
by the Romans. This may be true, but posterity has given the
credit to the Romans and we shall continue to think in terms
of Roman roads.

The Saxons avoided these roads. Some roads came back into use later and, indeed, part of the one from Buxton to Little Chester must still have been in use in 1738 when the trustees of the Loughborough–Derby–Brassington turnpike decided to end their road northward at the remote, obscure hamlet of Hurdlow instead of continuing to Buxton. Clearly this decision could only have been made because the next section of what was the main London–Manchester road required no major improvements. Today the A515 still follows the line of this Roman road between Hurdlow and Buxton with only minor deviations.

As early as 1725 an Act had been obtained 'to amend the dangerous, narrow, and at times impassable road from Buxton, through Chapel-en-le-Frith to Manchester'. This, the first turnpike road in the Peak, is now once again the main Manchester road, though it has only recently acquired the label A6 in preference to the road that drops in a series of hairpin bends to the Goyt Valley at Whaley Bridge. The rest of the present A6 northwards from Derby developed piecemeal. It was not completed until 1818 when a narrow passageway was blasted through the solid limestone at Scarthin Nick to open up a new approach to the Matlock gorge from the south and form an important junction with the Wirksworth–Alfreton road that ran east and west across the grain of the country.

A hundred yards or so west of Scarthin Nick, beyond Cromford Market Place, the Wirksworth road was joined by a new road built about 1800 by Philip Gell of Hopton to link his lead mines at Carsington to a smelting house at Cromford and the wharf at the terminus of the Cromford Canal. Gell called his road through the lovely Griffe Grange Valley the Via Gellia, 'an affectation that may be pardoned', wrote the Rev Richard Warner, travelling along the road shortly after it was opened, 'as it contributes much to the enjoyment and comfort of the traveller, conducting him through a shorter,

116

more agreeable and convenient route than the former one'. Perhaps the name was as much a deliberate piece of symbolism as of pretentiousness because the Gells half accepted a tradition of Roman ancestry and because it may have occurred to Philip Gell that his was, with one exception, the first piece of deliberate road construction in the Peak—as distinct from the early tinkerings of the turnpike trusts—since Roman times. The single exception was at Chatsworth, where in 1761 Capability Brown planned the present north–south road through the park from Baslow to Beeley to replace the old road that dropped steeply down from the East Moor and climbed almost equally tediously up the western slopes of the park.

But the achievements of the turnpike trusts should not be underestimated. In 1784 George Augustus Walpole found it 'a matter of no great difficulty' to visit Chatsworth because of 'the good turnpike roads now everywhere about it', whereas a mere half century earlier that most ludicrous of Poet Laureates, Colley Cibber, 'thought I should have broke my neck' to get there. Many stretches of turnpike road are still in use, though often now as minor roads, and many of the milestones that were made compulsory under the General Turnpike Acts of 1766 and 1773 still decorate the roadside verges, there being at least three on the old road between Conksbury Bridge and the Newhaven Hotel. A few toll houses have also survived, like the one on the Sheffield road on the outskirts of Baslow. Another, on the Bakewell to Great Longstone road, has been modernised, but proclaims its origin in a rebus in the form of a bell and a gate on its gable. Some inns too were built to serve travellers on the turnpike roads. One obvious example is the lonely, gaunt Newhaven Hotel on the A515. Built by the fifth Duke of Devonshire around 1800, with stabling for a hundred horses, it was, according to J. B. Firth, placed above the licensing laws by George IV who granted the Duke a 'free and perpetual licence' in return for a pleasant evening's entertainment there, though nowadays it seems to conform to orthodox licensing hours. The sixth Duke, who also had an eye for a good site, built the Snake Inn in 1821 on the then newly-built Manchester–Sheffield turnpike that replaced the older, longer route through Whaley Bridge, Chapel-en-le-Frith, Sparrowpit and Hathersage. This Snake Road, and the inn, take their name not from the road's sinuous windings but from the snake on the Cavendish armorial bearings.

The Snake was the last important turnpike road to be built in the Peak. With its completion and the addition of a few enclosure roads with their wide grass verges—like several round Monyash—the road network took on the shape that, give or take a short stretch of bypass or two, exists today. Between 1725 and 1825 a revolution had taken place in Peakland communications. In 1829 a local historian reported that there were still people living in Ashover who could remember when there was neither cart nor wagon in the village, 'and there were several other villages where a wagon could not be taken because of the steepness of the hills'.

In such a hilly area the pack-horse was the only means of carrying heavy goods 'across the moors and dales'. A traveller in 1755 commented on 'the vast number of pack-horses travelling over the hills, of which (between Buxton and Matlock Bath) we counted sixty in a drove; their chief loading is wood and malt, which they carry across the county from Nottingham and Derby to Manchester'. The men accompanying these pack-horse convoys were known locally as 'jaggers', and names like Jaggers Clough and numerous Jaggers Lanes give some indication of the route they followed, just as Saltersford, and the fairly common Salters Lane and Salter Gate, tell of the old salt routes eastward from the Cheshire Plain. That one such salt route followed Longdendale may explain why that long thin finger of territory belonged to Cheshire until 1974.

The pack-horse trains were sometimes replaced by 'cumbersome wains drawn by oxen', according to an early-nineteenth-century writer, but the horse-drawn wagon or cart became common as roads improved. 'In the High Peak', says the same writer, 'carts were drawn by two or three or even four horses and furnished with a strong drag chain fastened to the top of the hind part of the cart. The carter would lead his horses down the hill with the drag chain dragging on the ground.'

The movement of heavy goods continued to pose a problem in the Peak, where the gradients defeated even Brindley and his fellow canal builders. The only canals constructed in the area were the Peak Forest in the extreme north-west and the Cromford in the south-east, with the Macclesfield Canal just touching the western fringe. The Peak Forest Canal ran from Bugsworth—altered in 1930 to Buxworth at the request of those inhabitants who could not take the jokes—for 14 miles to join the Manchester, Ashton and Oldham Canal and so carry goods into the heart of Manchester. Another short arm from Whaley Bridge joined the main line just north of Buxworth. Samuel Oldknow and Richard Arkwright were among those who pressed for the canal, which was obviously useful for serving the cotton mills. Benjamin Outram was its engineer and he was responsible for the flight of 16 locks and 'that grandest of all aqueducts' that filled the young George Borrow's 'mind with wonder' when he first saw it spanning the Goyt. Both these are near Marple. The aqueduct is now itself dominated by an even more impressive railway viaduct.

Outram also worked on the Cromford Canal, but under the supervision of the more experienced William Jessop, one of his three partners in the foundation of the Butterley Ironworks in 1792. The canal, completed in the following year, tunnels immediately under the ironworks, which lies on the Coal Measures just east of the Peak. Where the canal turns eastwards at Bull Bridge, Jessop built a 200yd long aqueduct of shale freestone to cross the river Amber and a main road. In 1839 another insertion was made in the embankment, and the canal encased in an iron trough, to permit the passage of the North Midland Railway's main York–Derby line. Unfortunately this splendid aqueduct was demolished in 1968 to permit road widening, but there is another fine one of the same length at Wigwell, over the Derwent, a few miles farther north. At its north end is the Leawood pumphouse, a handsome gritstone building with a tall chimney. The beam engine inside, built in 1849, was used to pump water from the Derwent to the canal until the canal was abandoned in 1944. Thirty years later the Cromford Canal Society restored the engine, and it can now be seen in working order in its pumphouse.

This restoration, heartening enough in itself, is only part of the story of a 'kiss of life' revival of two canals that were seemingly dead. Both, after half a century or so of vigorous life that did much to bring prosperity to their respective hinterlands, were taken over by railway companies: the Peak Forest by the Manchester, Sheffield and Lincolnshire Railway—an ancestor of the Great Central—and the Cromford by the Manchester, Buxton, Matlock and Midland Junction Railway. Both canals were then allowed, through lack of maintenance, to fall gently into disuse and decay. But in 1968 volunteers began to restore Buxworth Basin. By 1974 the Peak Forest Canal had been restored from Marple to Dukinfield and was reopened for pleasure cruising. Such a completely happy ending was impossible for the Cromford Canal. The section between Ambergate and its junction with the Erewash Canal at Langley Mill was blocked by subsidence in Butterley Tunnel. But in 1974 the British Waterways Board handed over the vastly more attractive $5\frac{1}{2}$ mile stretch from Ambergate to its northern terminus, opposite Sir Richard Arkwright's original mill at Cromford, for use as, in planning

Page 121 *(above)* Ashopton Viaduct, Ladybower Reservoir in the upper Derwent Valley; *(below)* Eldon Hill Quarry

Page 122 Hummocks of leadmine waste on Longstone Edge mark the course of Tideslow Rake

jargon, an 'amenity waterway'. The restoration of the Lea-wood pumphouse and engine was just the first step towards bringing back this idyllically beautiful stretch of waterway to something like its former glory.

Unfortunately the tramroads that linked these canals with various quarries and other works and played such a vital part in the economic life of the Peak are beyond restoration, though traces of many can still be detected by knowledgeable industrial archaeologists. Some of these tramroads—virtually narrow-gauge railways—were built by Outram, giving rise to the myth, still firmly believed by many Derbyshire people despite much scholarly debunking, that the name 'tram' was derived from the last syllable in Outram.

He certainly built what was one of the most spectacular and useful of all these canal feeder lines: The Peak Forest Limestone Tramway. Opened in 1796, it carried limestone and lime from the quarries and kilns at Dove Holes down to the canal basin at Buxworth 6 miles away. 'Down' is the operative word. For most of the journey the train of wagons was propelled by gravity, though horses—some thirty in all—were used on the level stretches. Teams of horses hauled the wagons from the quarries to the highest point on the line. When the horses were unhitched the brakeman gave the 'gang' of wagons—varying between 16 and 40—a push which started it on its steady run down a 1 in 60 gradient to marshalling yards above Chapel-en-le-Frith. Then came a descent on a 1 in 7 gradient by means of an inclined plane. No more than 8 wagons at a time were allowed on this and their weight was employed to pull up empty wagons, using a wire rope that ran round an 18ft wide wooden drum. The whole operation was controlled by a man in a lighthouse-like control tower, but there were times when the wagons ran out of control, jumped the rails and scattered their loads. The gangs that safely negotiated the incline were reassembled and, using their own momentum once more, were dispatched

H

on the final 2 mile run to Buxworth Basin, where the freight was tipped into canal boats. The whole journey took up to 3 hours, much time being lost on the inclined plane. But not all the problems arose there; the gravity sections had their perils, especially for the brakeman. He rode uncomfortably on the outside of a truck and if the gang gathered too much speed, as often happened when they were fully loaded, he could apply a crude brake. This was an iron pin on the end of a short chain which hung by each pair of wheels. The brakeman had to bend down and insert the pin between the iron spokes of the wheel into a socket, thus locking the wheels. If this failed to take off enough speed he would have to clamber from wagon to wagon repeating the operation. Surprisingly few brakemen ever seem to have been seriously injured.

The tramway, which gave a considerable boost to Dove Holes as a quarrying centre and Buxworth as an inland port, continued in use—under railway ownership from 1846—until 1920. Some of the stone sleepers and portions of the raised cobbled path that was laid between the rails to give a firm grip for the horses still lie under thick grass. A few examples of wagon and Outram's typical L-shaped flanged rail are in the railway museums at York and Towyn.

Outram probably also built the tramway that ran from Hilts Quarry at Crich to the Cromford Canal wharf at Bull Bridge, but its most remarkable, though short-lived feature, was introduced after his death. This was Brunton's Walking Locomotive, a sort of 'daddy long-legs' contraption that steamed at a speed of 2½mph on what were virtually stilts. Built at Butterley in 1813, it performed tolerably well until 1815 when a sister engine in use at Newcastle Colliery in Durham burst its boiler, killing 11 people. The Crich locomotive was then withdrawn from service.

Of slightly later vintage was the line that George Stephenson built from Crich Cliff Quarry to his battery of lime kilns at Ambergate. It was in use from 1842 until 1957 and the line of its gravity-incline of 1 in 7 can still be seen.

It is a strange coincidence that Crich Cliff Quarry has been since 1959 the home of the Tramway Museum, where visitors may see and ride on tram cars brought from places as far apart as Sheffield and Johannesburg, Glasgow and Vienna, suitably decorated, like the workshops and other buildings, with nostalgic Edwardian advertisements. If this village home may seem a somewhat bizarre setting in which to preserve such a typically urban product as the tram car, it should be remembered that the vehicle's direct ancestor was the canal feeder wagon and that Matlock, only 4 miles away, once claimed to have the steepest passenger-carrying tramway in the world. This carried passengers up the hill from Crown Square, in the town centre, to Smedley's Hydro, half a mile away. Built at the instigation of the Matlock-born Sir George Newnes, the publisher, in 1893, it was bought by him in 1898 and presented to the town. It had only three cars, carrying 31 passengers each, which were hauled up and down the 1 in $5\frac{1}{2}$ gradient. After losing money steadily for some years, the line closed in 1927. A week later the single cable snapped. The gritstone engine house and tramway shed still stand at the top of the hill, and a delightfully Emett-like shelter now graces the nearby riverside gardens.

The Tramway Museum, interesting and worthy as it is, and the eccentric Matlock tramway, play only minor roles in the story of communications in the Peak. The real link between the age of canals and their feeder tramways and the age of railways was the Cromford and High Peak Railway, which also linked the Cromford Canal with the Peak Forest, a distance, as the train travelled, of just over 33 miles.

The original concept was to cross the central watershed of England by means of a canal that would connect the network of waterways based on the Trent with Manchester and the waterways of the north-west, providing also an outlet for lime, other minerals and agricultural products and an inward flow of coal to remote areas. But faced with the task of building the almost innumerable locks to raise the waterway on to the plateau of the White Peak and the problem of maintaining sufficient water in a limestone region, the promoters decided in 1823 to substitute a railway. Josias Jessop, William's son, was appointed engineer. His estimate of £155,080 proved to be about £25,000 short of the mark. An Act of 1825 empowered the company to construct a railway or tramroad on which wagons were to be 'propelled by stationary or locomotive engines or other sufficient power' between Cromford and Whaley Bridge. The first section from Cromford to the summit level of 1,264ft at Hurdlow, opened on 29 May 1830, used five inclined planes worked by stationary engines; the second section to the terminus at Whaley Bridge had four inclined planes, three of them worked by stationary engines but the final descent to 517ft at Whaley Bridge used the counterbalance system. 'The other sufficient power' on the fairly level portions was provided by horses until locomotives took over in 1841, though some horses continued to be used for the next decade or so.

The railway became 'one of the thoroughfares of England', according to an early railway historian, Francis Williams, but it was always in financial trouble. Short extensions in the 1850s from Cromford Wharf to High Peak Junction, to connect with the MBM & MJR, and at Whaley Bridge, to form a link with the Stockport, Disley & Whaley Bridge Railway, brought only marginal improvements. The experiment of carrying pasengers, begun in 1833, was abandoned after an accident in 1877. A half-crown single fare from Cromford to Buxton, with a coach connection at Ladmanlow, brought little money to the company and a lesson in patience for the passengers, who had to walk up the inclines and be prepared to wait for an engine at the top of Middleton Incline. A friend of Williams was told he might have to wait five minutes there, or a few hours. 'It all depends', the guard told him, 'when the engine comes to take you on. Yesterday it didn't come at all.' Williams' friend was moderately fortunate; the engine arrived some three hours later. The whole journey took six hours.

In 1861 the London and North Western Railway leased the line and took it over completely in 1887, when the C & HP company was dissolved. The section northward from Parsley Hay was absorbed into the LNWR Ashbourne–Buxton branch line in 1892 and the Ladmanlow–Whaley Bridge section was abandoned, except for the short final stretch—including the Whaley Bridge inclined plane, which continued in use for another 60 years. The abandoned section included the two Bunsal inclines that lowered the line into the Goyt Valley. These inclines, with gradients of 1 in 7 and 1 in $7\frac{1}{2}$ were the steepest on the entire line. It now seems to have been established by W. H. Hoult that J. B. Fell's experimental work on mountain railways in the 1860s was carried out on a stretch of line that passed under the Bunsal incline.

Between Cromford and Parsley Hay the C & HP continued in use—mainly carrying stones from the quarries—until 2 October 1967. Today, bereft of its rails, it has become the Derbyshire County Council's High Peak Trail, linking up with the Peak Park Board's Tissington Trail at Parsley Hay to give 17 miles of pleasing bridleway, with several features of special interest to railway enthusiasts, including the workshop at High Peak Junction and a catch pit nearby at the foot of Sheep Pasture Incline, installed after runaway trucks had leaped the A6 and the canal. Further up the trail, near Friden, is a series of remarkably sharp curves, the one at Gotham of $2\frac{1}{2}$ chains radius being the most acute on any railway in Britain. Nearby, the 1 in 14 Hopton Incline was the steepest incline in Britain to be worked by locomotives. The portals of Newhaven Tunnel under the A515 road are adorned with plaques bearing the company's name round a wagon, the contractor's initials and the date 1825, the crest of the company and the names of the engineer and clerk. But of more general interest is the octagonal engine house at the summit of Middleton Incline, containing the original beam engine built at Butterley in 1825 and used continuously to wind trucks up the incline until 1967. For most of that time it was worked by successive generations of the Spencer family. Since the line closed, both the engine house and the winding engine have been restored and may be seen by the public on Sundays.

Though the Cromford and High Peak Railway brought benefit to the mineral interests in the White Peak it did little to ease communications between Manchester and the East Midlands. That the link between these two thriving industrial regions was not forged until 1867 was due less to the undoubted engineering problems than to the obduracy of the Dukes of Devonshire and Rutland, whose vast neighbouring estates blocked the line of advance north of Rowsley. The railway reached that point in two stages. The first section, to Ambergate, was part of George Stephenson's North Midland Railway which connected Derby with Leeds. Completed in 1840, it was notable for its fine stations by Francis Thompson, the only survivor of which is a rather dejected South Wingfield, but this line touches the Peak only at Ambergate, where Stephenson's Toadmoor Tunnel of gritstone had to be given an unusual flat arch—now reinforced by steel hoops—to prevent landslips of slippery shale. From Ambergate to Rowsley the line was carried forward in 1849 by the optimistically named Manchester, Buxton, Matlock & Midland Junction Railway, which failed to reach Manchester, or for that matter, Buxton, before being leased jointly to the rival Midland and London and North Western railways in 1852 and absorbed into the Midland system in 1871.

It was the Midland that inherited duke trouble. Like many other landowners, neither Devonshire nor Rutland was enthusiastic about having a railway line through his estate. But the sixth Duke of Devonshire, probably influenced by Sir Joseph Paxton—who designed the original Rowsley Station and possibly four of the terraced houses nearby that are still called Midland Cottages—eventually agreed to allow the line to pass through Chatsworth Park so long as it was under cove₁. Unfortunately, he died before any action could be taken, and his successor would not have the railway on any conditions. Eventually, after much haggling, the Duke of Rutland agreed that the line could be carried through his estate under cover along the hillside at the back of Haddon Hall instead of along the valley bottom as the engineers had hoped. And there were other restrictions, as Francis Williams pointed out.

> A thousand special precautions had to be observed. None of the trees were to be removed or lopped; agents and keepers were set to watch the property and the game; one duke wanted the principal station to be at Bakewell, and the other required that it should be at Hassop, and both had to be built; and the line through the park of Haddon Hall was carried along the hillside by the excavation of portions—half cutting, half tunnel—which were then covered in.

The covering of Haddon Tunnel is only 8ft thick in places. During construction it collapsed, and 5 men died.

This was not the only accident during the building of this line that created so many engineering problems. The first problem lay in finding a site for a new station at Rowsley because the deviation into the Wye Valley necessitated bypassing the original station, which survives today as a road-haulage office. Beyond Haddon there were innumerable crossings of the Wye—most spectacularly by the Monsal viaduct, which gave no particular trouble when building but had to be extensively repaired after a minor landslip in 1907—and by frequent tunnels through limestone which was sometimes less solid than it appeared. During the construction of Dove Holes tunnel, the longest on this line, the work-men struck an underground river. This was diverted, but reappeared. Again it was diverted, apparently successfully, but it may have been the cause of the tunnel collapsing in 1870. There was a further collapse after heavy rain in February 1940. This nearly caused a major disaster. A south-bound train ran into the rubble without serious damage, and its guard raced through the tunnel in time to stop an approaching north-bound goods train from entering. Further repairs kept 80 workmen busy nightly for $2\frac{1}{2}$ years in the 1950s.

Despite the various hazards the line was apparently ready for opening on 1 November 1866 when a landslip occurred at Buxworth. This put the opening back by 3 months. But on 1 February 1867 the passenger service between London and Manchester opened along one of the country's most attractive and exciting lines.

Buxton had received the benefit of railway four years earlier. A luncheon in the splendid Assembly Rooms in the Crescent on Saturday 30 May 1863 celebrated what should have been the simultaneous arrival on the following Monday of new railways from two directions: the Stockport, Disley and Whaley Bridge Railway from the north-west and the Midland from the south-east. To receive them were two new stations side by side and outwardly identical, having both been designed by Paxton. So far as the SD & WBR were concerned the celebrations were slightly premature, as their line did not open until 15 June, but the Midland arrived triumphantly on 1 June by way of what was destined to be a branch line from Miller's Dale but was for the next four years, before the completion of the Manchester section, the terminus of the line from Derby.

Much was made at the luncheon of the Duke of Devon-shire's generosity in promoting both railways although it would result in the loss of virtually all his revenue from the turnpike road south of Buxton, but as the duke then owned practically all Buxton, which boomed as a holiday resort after the coming of the railways, it seems that he was merely transferring the revenue from one pocket to another larger one. Buxton's tourist traffic received a further fillip when the LNWR opened its branch from Ashbourne in 1899— with a loop to the old SD & WBR line at Whaley Bridge— during the second period of 'railway mania'. This was an attempt to outsmart the Midland by running a main line from Euston to Manchester via Buxton as well as to tap the milk trade from Peakland farms. From the LNWR point of view it was an unsuccessful move, although through trains ran from Euston to Buxton, via Nuneaton and Ashbourne, until 1917 and a milk train to Finsbury Park daily until after World War II. But it brought into Buxton additional tourists, particularly day excursionists from Manchester and Liverpool, and added two impressive features to the Buxton landscape: a viaduct of 15 arches across the Wye Valley and the town, and another, even more impressive, crossing the road known as Duke's Drive. These new 'wonders' apart, the section of line between Buxton and Parsley Hay involved nothing more than a reconstruction of the old C & HP line and was fully operational in 1894. But south of Parsley Hay the going was tougher. Half a mile of solid limestone had to be blasted away with gelignite to make a cutting 60ft deep near Parsley Hay station. The 7-arched viaduct between Ashbourne and Thorpe involved the removal of more than 200,000 cubic yards of boulder clay. Workmen preparing the foundations of the Hand Dale viaduct near Hartington opened up old mine workings containing skeletons of men who had been trapped there long before. And finding sleeping accommodation for the 500 navvies was an almost insoluble problem. Many of them slept rough in the new Ashbourne station that was being built jointly by the LNWR and North Staffordshire Railways—for the latter's Churnet Valley line to Rocester—

overlooking the garden where Dr Johnson used to stroll with his host Dr Taylor.

The story of Peakland railways is indeed one of engineering wonders and of the tough, hard-drinking men who built them. The building of the first Woodhead Tunnel was described by a contemporary as 'a wonderous triumph of art over nature', and much later by Terry Coleman as 'the most degraded adventure of the navvy age'. There were three Woodhead tunnels, and the building of the first two—'a story of heroic savagery, magnificent profits, and devout hypocrisy'—has been definitively told by Terry Coleman. All that need be stated here are the bare details of the building of the first purely locomotive-operated railway in the Peak, and the first railway link between Sheffield and Manchester.

The Sheffield, Ashton-under-Lyne and Manchester Railway built their line through the Pennines between 1838 and 1845. It involved the construction of the spectacular Dinting Vale viaduct which now bears the weight of 1,000 ton goods trains, its 5 original 125ft centre arches of timber having been replaced by steel ones. But the Woodhead Tunnel was the major undertaking. Just over 3 miles long, it was then the longest railway tunnel in the world. It took 6 years to build, and at times more than 1,500 men worked on it simultaneously. The cost was about £200,000; rather more than three times the original estimate. The casualty list included 33 workmen killed, 140 seriously injured—including 97 with fractures—and more than 400 slightly injured. It had been, as was said at the celebratory dinner at the Cutlers' Hall in Sheffield two nights before Christmas 1845, 'a very stiff job'.

Eighteen months later, work started on the second tunnel. Originally the first had been planned to take a double line of track, but a late decision was made to economise with a narrower tunnel for a single line. This proved to be false economy. Woodhead became a bottleneck. The railway company—by then the Manchester, Sheffield and Lincolnshire Railway—found themselves compelled to drive a second bore. Because the engineers of the first tunnel had foreseen the need for a second one and had driven 25 arches at 200yd intervals into the side walls, the work was easier, cheaper and less dangerous. The job was completed in less than 5 years and casualties were fewer, but 28 men died from cholera in the summer of 1849, having picked up the germ on a drinking spree in Ashton. Their graves may be seen in the churchyards at Penistone, Woodhead, Tintwhistle and Mottram-in-Longdendale.

The Woodhead tunnel acquired a reputation as a graveyard for railwaymen. No train crews died from suffocation in this pitch-black, sulphur-filled rabbit hole under the Pennines, but many were only saved by the sensible precaution of breathing through wet rags, and conditions were little better for passengers. Gangers, it was said, developed pneumonosilicosis in less than 6 years. Nevertheless, the twin tunnels continued in use until 1954 when a third was built to carry the new electrified trans-Pennine line. The two earlier tunnels were then closed, but, as already mentioned, the second one was reopened to carry the electrical supergrid on its way from Thorpe Marsh near Doncaster to Stalybridge in Cheshire, a project that was completed in 1970. In that same year the third tunnel was closed to passenger traffic, though mineral trains still thunder through.

Passengers between Sheffield and Manchester now use the atractive Hope Valley line, opened by the Midland Railway in 1894—after more tunnel trouble. Totley Tunnel links the Sheaf and Derwent valleys; Cowburn burrows under the western watershed near the head of the Vale of Edale. Totley was the difficult one. The problem was not just its length— at 3 miles 950yd it is Britain's second longest railway tunnel —but water, the curse of most engineering projects in the Peak, though here the rock was not limestone but Millstone

Grit and shale. As a contemporary wrote, '. . . if the persons in charge of Totley tunnel had wished to tap every spring in the hill they could not have done it more successfully'. For 8 months in 1889 water was pumped from the workings at the rate of $2\frac{1}{4}$ million gallons a day, but on really bad days the rate rose to over 5 million a day. Cowburn was, literally, more straightforward. It runs dead straight for its entire 2 miles, and though at one time water 90ft deep collected in the shaft, men working in diving bells were able to complete the job in a mere 3 years.

With the completion of this line and the Buxton–Ashbourne line, the railway network across the Peak was virtually finished. The Leek & Manifold Railway (see Chapter 6) was a short-lived product of the period of Light Railway 'mania' in the first decade of this century. The Ashover Light Railway was an unexpectedly late arrival in 1925, but it survived for only 25 years. It was built by the Clay Cross Company to connect their ironworks at Clay Cross, east of the Peak, with their lead mines and fluorspar workings at Ashover $7\frac{1}{2}$ miles away, but it proved popular with tourists and developed a useful passenger service until the arrival of more convenient bus services. All the engines employed in the line were named after members of the Jackson family who had owned the Clay Cross firm since Robert Stephenson resigned in 1851, three years after his father's death. It seems appropriate that the last railway to come to the Peak should have been built by a firm founded by George Stephenson.

In the heyday of the railways between 1905 and 1935 some 145 miles of track crossed the Peak, doing much to open up the quarrying and mineral industries, providing a valuable outlet for agricultural products and a useful link with the outside world for the inhabitants. But some stations were a considerable distance from the villages they aimed to serve. Peak Forest was 3 miles from the tiny village of that name, Hassop 2 miles from its village, and Hartington $1\frac{1}{2}$ miles uphill from that charming tourist centre. But most people even in the more remote parts of the area were within five miles or so of a railway station.

That is not so today. In 1971 there were only 81 miles of railway in the Peak, of which a mere 57 carried passengers. The Hope Valley line is still in use, and there is a good commuter service between Buxton and Manchester. But southward the position is much bleaker. Ashbourne and Wirksworth are no longer served by rail. Between Matlock, the terminus of a branch from Derby, and the Hope Valley there is no rail service of any kind. Passengers from Derby to Manchester have to go by way of Dore and the Hope Valley line. The Ashbourne–Buxton line is now a green bridleway, thought up by the Peak Park Board on the sound conservationist grounds that it was infinitely preferable to an ugly scar running across the Park.

To encourage its use—and to entice people to leave their cars at home—the Board have introduced the Peak Pathfinder bus service linking up the sites of the now demolished stations on Sundays and Bank Holidays from Easter to late September.

Keeping out the motor car is something that exercises the minds of the local planners, necessarily if the roads of the Peak are not to seize up under the sheer volume of traffic. Though many roads are quiet there are places that already suffer from automobile inflation, with too many chasing too little road space and, particularly, too few parking spaces. The problem has already been tackled in various ways: the Pathfinder service, the provision of new car parks along the two trails, the Goyt Valley experiment and the projected ban on cars north of Edale—except for access to the farms— and in the Winnats Pass. This last scheme is an interesting example of conflict and compromise between planners and local people. The Winnats west of Castleton, is a steep, dry dale through which ran the turnpike road to Sparrowpit. Now a gridded by-road, it remained a popular short cut for local motorists and a popular parking spot for visitors to the local caves, to the detriment of the grass verges and the discomfort of walkers. The Peak Board decided to close the road to motorists. The locals objected strongly. Finally it was decided to close the road on summer weekends for a trial period.

Other ideas are being mooted. One would segregate the lorries from the cars by widening some of the less attractive minor roads as commercial routes and encouraging private motorists to avoid them. Subsidised bus services are being discussed and would be especially welcomed on the west side of the Peak, as would a combined bus/mail service. More ambitious is the proposal put forward by local railway enthusiasts and supported, so far rather tepidly, by the Peak Park Board, to reopen the Derby–Manchester railway line. The cost would be nearly £2 million according to a 1974 estimate, about half of which would go to restore a recently demolished bridge at Rowsley, the only major engineering undertaking—apart from relaying the track—that would be required.

Not all these schemes may come to fruition, but some—and perhaps others not yet considered—must if the Peak is to be saved from the menace of the motor car.

8 INDUSTRY

ALL the major industries in the Peak spring basically from what Sir John Betjeman called the 'stone'. The rocks, the soil that rubbed off them, the minerals that were found with them and the shapes that the rocks assumed created the wealth—some natives would put that word in inverted commas—on which the people of the Peak have been dining out, so to say, ever since. Quarrying, the extraction of fluorspar and other minerals, agriculture and tourism are the honey from the rocks. So, too, was lead mining.

It is odd that so many people still think of lead mining as the Peak's principal industry though it has not been that for at least a century. In 1861 there were 2,333 lead miners in the White Peak and its immediate fringes; perhaps half as many as a century earlier. By 1881 the number had shrunk to 871, and 20 years later to a mere 285. It is doubtful now if one could find half a dozen men scraping a living out of the ground in this way. But there seems to be a feeling that the industry is not dead but merely sleeping, like Arthur and his knights in British folklore, waiting to be awakened in the hour of the nation's need, and perfectly staid mining experts have said publicly that there is as much lead ore still lying untapped under the Derbyshire Dome as has been extracted in the last thousand years. And if lead miners are hard to find, there are plenty of men around who can tell their stowe from their stemple and can converse happily in the strangely archaic jargon of the industry. Though the visitor to the Peak does not have to know about buddling,

cat dirt, kibbles or slickensides, he should have some knowledge of rakes, scrins, flats, pipes and T'Owd Man.

A rake is a main vein of minerals filling what is normally
an almost vertical fissure in the limestone. It is virtually a
wall of minerals up to twenty feet wide and five hundred
feet or more deep, sometimes, like Long Rake near Arbor Low,
or Dirtlow Rake near Castleton, running for several miles
across country, its course plainly marked by grass-covered
hillocks of waste from old mines. Scrins are mini-rakes, but
as nobody has ever defined when a scrin is big enough to be
called a rake the names are pretty well interchangeable.
Distinguishing between flats and pipes presents similar
problems; the distinction is as subtle as that between the
working and lower middle class in the English caste system.
Flats are mineral deposits lying almost horizontally between
separate limestone strata. Length and breadth are usually
about equal; up to half a mile across with a thickness of up
to twenty feet or thereabouts. Pipes are long, thin veins, as
the name suggests, but of course you can have fairly short
pipes which could be flats.

T'Owd Man is even more confusing because he can be
almost all things to all men. He can be the personification of
the mine itself, or the ore, or the hummock of waste, or even
the spirit of miners, long dead. Whatever he is, his name
crops up often in Peakland pubs.

If the language of lead mining is odd, so, too, are its laws
and customs. These are based on the rulings of the Inquisition
for the King's Field of the High Peak held at Ashbourne
in 1288, but this inquiry undoubtedly drew on established
precedents which may have gone back to Saxon times or
even earlier. For mining purposes the area is divided into
liberties, comprising groups of parishes or a single parish.
The laws vary slightly from liberty to liberty, but those for
the High Peak—which for mining purposes included Monyash, Castleton, Winster and Bradwell among other places—

Page 139 (above) Stone walls and sheep on the limestone uplands, Longstone Edge; (right) river Wye in Monsal Dale

Page 140 Coffin-lid, probably of seventh-century Celtic missionary, Wirksworth Church

are fairly typical. Each liberty had a barmaster who was—and still is—the representative of the Crown responsible for the administration of mining law. With certain exceptions, such as churchyards, gardens, orchards and highways, it was 'lawful for all the King's liege people to dig, delve, search, subvert and turn all manner of grounds, lands, meadows, closes, pastures, meres and marshes' for lead ore, regardless of the feelings of landowners. Once a vein had been discovered, and 'freed', or registered, by the barmaster, the miner had the right of access to the nearest highway, but for horse transport only and not for 'wayn or sled' except by agreement. The width of this mine road was usually decided by the barmaster and two jurymen of the Barmote Court walking abreast with arms outstretched and finger-tips touching.

Once the miner had been granted possession of his mine he had to erect a stowe (or windlass), which was in effect his title deed. In practice, the model of a stowe was sufficient to show possession, but this had to be kept standing while the mine was working. If the mine stood idle for three weeks—except because of flooding or ventilation problems—the barmaster could 'nick' the stowe by cutting a notch in it. This nicking would be repeated twice more, usually at three-weekly intervals. If the mine was still unworked after the third nicking it was forfeited and the stowe thrown down.

Expulsion from the liberty was often the punishment for poaching on another miner's vein. Stealing ore was dealt with even more harshly in the Low Peak. Two offences merited fines; for a third offence the thief had his hand nailed to the stowe by a knife, as well as losing all mining rights.

This particular punishment has lapsed, but lead mining laws are still administered, as they have been for nearly 700 years, by the Great Barmote courts, usually consisting of 24 jurors presided over by the Queen's Barmaster. The Court

of the King's Field of the Low Peak still meets twice a year
in the Moot Hall at Wirksworth to settle mining disputes
in the Wapentake of Wirksworth. If the business of the court
nowadays sometimes occupies less time than the adjournment
to consume lunch with punch, its rights are still jealously
guarded. The hint dropped in 1973 that it might be abolished
in a legal tidying up operation by the Lord Chancellor was
greeted by such opposition that the idea of closing what
must be some of Britain's oldest courts was quietly forgotten.

But even the courts are fairly modern by the standards of
an industry that goes back to Roman times and probably
earlier. It is not possible to say of any Peakland mine that it
was definitely worked in Roman times, but the Nestus Mine
on Masson Hill, Matlock, and now known to tourists as
Rutland Cavern, and other commercial 'caves' at Matlock
could have Roman origins. Proof that the Romans worked
lead in the area rests mainly on the fifteen pigs of lead
that have turned up in various parts of Britain, including
Cromford, Nether Moor, Matlock Bank, Tansley Moor and
Bradwell in Derbyshire. Each pig has stamped on it an
abbreviated form of the name Lutudarum, which must have
been a centre of the industry at that time, unless it was the
name of the company that controlled the mines.

The exact whereabouts of Lutudarum, if it was a place,
has never been firmly established, although claims have been
made for Matlock, Chesterfield, Wirksworth or even the
whole of the White Peak. Certainly in Defoe's time, and for
at least 1,000 years before that, Wirksworth was 'a kind of
market for lead; the like not known anywhere else that I
know of, except it be the custom house keys in London'.
It was from Wirksworth that an eighth-century Abbess of
Repton sent lead to Crowland Abbey for St Guthlac's coffin,
and a little later some for the roof of Canterbury Cathedral.
Inside the Moot Hall, a plain building of 1814, is an oblong
brass dish, holding 14pt, that was used as a standard measure

for lead ore within the Wapentake—itself a splendid name that has survived from Danish times. The dish was made, according to the inscription round the rim, 'in the lllj yere of the reign of Kyng Henry the VIII, before George, Earle of Shrowesbury', and was to remain in the Moot Hall, 'so as the Merchauntes or mynours may resote to the same at all tymes to make the true measure after the same'.

It was round about the reign of Henry VIII that German mining engineers brought improved techniques to the Peak. The industry reached its heyday in the first half of the eighteenth century, helped by the introduction of the steam pumping engine, and after a slump during the Napoleonic Wars there was a brief revival in the period 1830–60 influenced by rising lead prices and an influx of new capital from larger companies into what had been essentially an under-capitalised industry run by working shareholders. But prices dropped again, and what seems to be the final crash came, hastened by the opening up of the rich, easily worked lead-zinc mines at Broken Hill in New South Wales.

Around the same time certain rich lead veins became exhausted, but the greatest single factor in the collapse of the lead-mining industry in the Peak was water in the mines. No major rake has ever been exploited to its full depth because of the cost and dangers involved in getting rid of the water that gushes below the Derbyshire Dome.

You can get a vivid picture of the lead miners' fight against water by going down into Lathkill Dale. Here, among the woods by the river, a mile or so from Over Haddon, you may find not only a mine shaft but the remains of a pumping house and the stone piers of an aqueduct used to drain Mandale Mine. There is evidence here of three attempts to drain the mine. First the Mandale Sough, a mile-long drainage channel that took 23 years to dig between 1797 and 1820. By the time it was finished the workings were already too low for it to be effective. The next step was to build an artificial leat, which carried water above the river to drive a water-wheel on the opposite bank. When this method of pumping proved ineffective, a Boulton & Watt steam pumping-engine was installed. But water won in the end and what you see down by the Lathkill are the remnants of a lost battle.

Another losing battle against water was fought out in the Mill Close Mine, Darley Dale, as late as 1938. In this, the largest and latest of Derbyshire mines, the 800 miners penetrated 900ft below the surface to raise annually over 30,000 tons of high-grade lead and over 10,000 tons of rich zinc sulphide, but each day they pumped out over 7 million gallons of water. Finally a sudden inrush overpowered the lowest pumps. Though the water was finally controlled and the mine pumped dry, mining was abandoned shortly afterwards when it became clear that to find a new vein of ore would involve the sinking of a new shaft and another immense pumping problem at a time of falling lead prices.

In earlier times, soughs were the miners' chief defence against flooding. These drainage channels carried the water—often from a network of mines—down to the nearest natural watercourse. They were costly to build. Cromford Sough had cost £30,000 when it was completed in 1688. Hill Carr Sough swallowed £50,000.

There are about seventy soughs in the Peak, but their tails (or outfalls) are not always easy to find, either because they are silted up and hidden by foliage, or because they are located on private property, like the tail of Calver Sough which emerges attractively in a cottage garden. But there is a fairly conspicuous outfall at Red Rake, ½ mile out of Calver on the Hassop road (SK 239741). The sough arch, dated 1851, has been preserved by the Peak District Mines Historical Society (founded 1958), which has also cleared much debris from the sough itself.

The promoters of Speedwell Mine, Castleton, deliberately

used the subterranean water system in the eighteenth century to transport waste rock and lead ore, an idea almost certainly introduced by John Gilbert, the mine agent, who had been the Duke of Bridgewater's land agent when James Brindley constructed his underground canal to the Duke's Worsley collieries. At the Speedwell Mine the main canals were in tunnels roughly seven feet high and wide, using water diverted from natural underground rivers. Men pushed the boats along the canals, using pegs driven into the walls of the tunnel at 6ft intervals. The mine was unsuccessful financially, but it has been a great tourist attraction since about 1800. Visitors today descend 104 concrete steps and are then pushed along in a boat for about half a mile to a platform built across the so-called Bottomless Pit Cavern, where they can see a lead vein and steps up to old workings.

Many other lead-mining relics are clearly visible on the limestone uplands. For instance, there are mine buildings at the Magpie Mine at Sheldon, which the PDMHS now use as a field centre, a conspicuous engine house of the New Engine Mine near Eyam, and a crushing wheel and its circular iron track at the Odin Mine—reputedly worked by the Danes—just by the A625 Castleton–Chapel-en-le-Frith road at the foot of Mam Tor. More ubiquitous are the miners' huts, or coes, many now roofless, where the workers stored their tools, and the lead ore awaiting inspection by the barmaster.

After inspection, the ore was carried, usually by pack-horse, to the smelting-mill; in its earliest form no more than a small stone hearth with a funnel-shaped mouth—insatiable in its demand for charcoal—set on the south-western side of a hill to catch the prevailing wind. Few, if any, of these 'boles' remain, though the locally common Bole Hill hints broadly at their sites. But a few ruins remain of the later cupolas, reverberatory furnaces fuelled by coal, that were introduced in the mid-eighteenth century. One on private ground among the trees by the Bradford just below Alport still has remnants of the underground flues, outbuildings and slagheaps half hidden in the long grass.

More dangerous relics are the uncovered mine shafts. There are 70,000 of them in the Peak. On Bradwell Moor, on Masson Hill above Matlock, round Monyash and Winster they riddle the ground. Some have been loosely covered by stones at some time or ringed around by ineffective fencing. Most, fortunately, are well off the beaten track, but they can still be a hazard to straying beasts and to the occasional over-venturesome walker, like the twelve-year-old boy who fell 80ft down an open shaft. He was comparatively lucky, brought up within the hour with only minor injuries, but his accident naturally raised the question of covering the shafts. This would cost about £4 million, the sort of money for which a local authority needs government grant aid. With this not yet forthcoming, the PDMHS has made a start on covering shafts on Masson with concrete caps that should be vandal-resistant and will avoid the need to fill in shafts that the Society—and many tourists—regard as interesting historical relics.

Some of the new holes that are appearing in the Peak District are made by miners of other minerals, especially fluorspar, calcium fluoride. Until about the turn of the century the lead miners regarded it in much the same way that too many visitors to Dovedale and other beauty spots regard the ice-cream carton or the cigarette packet: as useless material to be thrown down and left for nature to dispose of or hide. It had some small use in the making of hydrofluoric acid and in the manufacture of glass for church windows, but the miners seem to have largely disregarded this possible source of additional earnings. But when it was discovered, around 1900, that fluorspar was superior to limestone as a flux in the basic open-hearth method of steel making, the miners, with slightly red faces, began to rummage for it amongst their old workings.

Now the extraction of fluorspar has become a considerable industry in the Peak District. With many of the old workings thoroughly combed through, the mineral exploiters have turned to open-cast and underground mining, having discovered over the last half century many new uses for fluorspar. It is extensively used in the ceramics industry and in the extraction of aluminium from bauxite, and in various other industries. Above all, it has become a major raw material in the manufacture of steel and chemicals.

Today more than 200,000 tons of fluorspar are produced annually inside the Peak Park, mainly in a strip about a mile wide on the eastern fringe of the limestone area, roughly from Castleton and Bradwell in the north to Wirksworth and Matlock in the south. This amount represents nearly three-quarters of total British production of fluorspar. About one third of this is exported, bringing some £3 million a year into the national till, and with world demand growing at the rate of 8 per cent a year there is every prospect of export growth.

Economically, this is fine. Unfortunately, however, fluorspar working is a messy operation. The underground mining is not too objectionable—at least in the eyes of those who do not have to earn a living that way—though it does create a risk of subsidence in some areas. But the reworking of old spoil heaps and opencast mining, which between them produce about half the output, are more unsightly and destructive of the scenery. Great slices have been cut out of Longstone Edge, for instance, though modern mineral exploiters, more sensitive than were the old lead miners about restoring the land, have covered some of their gashes successfully.

Hiding the evidence of processing fluorspar is much more difficult. To produce fluorspar for the chemical industry the ore has to be extremely finely ground. Much of this grinding process is concentrated in the two largest processing plants in Britain; at Cavendish Mill, near Stoney Middleton, and at Hopton, which though just outside the Park is well within the Peak District. The waste material (or tailings) emerges from the plants in the form of a white slurry which is pumped into unsightly lagoons (or tailing dams). When one of the Cavendish Mill lagoons breached its walls some years ago, the slurry ran down Middleton Dale into Stoney Middleton village, causing alarm about the possible pollution of local streams. The wall has since been raised and strengthened to prevent further trouble, and some fairly successful attempts have been made at seeding and tree planting on filled lagoons. But if the industry continues to grow at its present rate tailings will swallow up an extra 7 acres of Peakland each year, rising to an annual 28 acres—the equivalent of 18 full-sized football pitches—by the end of the century unless the waste material can be made sufficiently stable to be disposed of in old mineral workings, or be put to some practical use.

The Peak's other minerals are less unsightly and less waste-ful of land. Barytes—barium sulphate, often called 'cawk' in Derbyshire—is extracted from veins to the west of the fluorspar area at the rate of about 20,000 tons a year. In the past its main uses have been for paint manufacture, tooth-paste and as a source of barium in the chemical industry, but it is now extensively used in drilling for North Sea oil. Calcite —calcium carbonate—is extracted from two mines at Long Rake near Youlgreave, and is used in the chemical industry, in stucco wall surfaces and in the mixture for painting white lines on roads. Heat-resistant silica bricks have been made at Friden, alongside the High Peak Trail, since the nine-teenth century, causing some eyebrow raising by tourists surprised to find brickmaking in progress in so remote a spot. But the choice of site was a good one, literally on top of a silica deposit—a mixture of sands, clays and quartzite pebbles that settled in pockets in the limestone—and right by the C & HPR, with a siding of its own. Nowadays most of its raw materials are imported, and arrive by lorry, but it still draws its labour from a scattered area on the west of the uplands where alternative employment, other than quarrying, is scarce.

Limestone quarrying is the largest user of labour in the Peak. It employs around 1,500 men within the National Park and at least as many again in the surrounding areas. Yet, surprisingly in what is decidedly a growth industry, employment has roughly halved over the last 30 years as a result of automation and mechanisation, while output has increased at the rate of 6 per cent a year. From the whole of the Derbyshire–Staffordshire limestone area about 20 million tons of limestone are extracted every year, roughly one-fifth of the total amount of limestone quarried in the whole of Britain.

Only about 6 million tons are produced from the 12 quarries within the Park each year, but many large quarries lie only just on the far side of the park fence, so to say, many of them within the Buxton–Chapel-en-le-Frith enclave that was deliberately excluded from the National Park. Among these is the ICI Tunstead quarry, the largest in the world outside the USA. From its $1\frac{1}{4}$ mile face, 200ft high in places, some 5 million tons of exceptionally pure limestone—98 per cent calcium carbonate—are extracted annually. Opened in 1929, this quarry has enough limestone left to meet demands until about the end of the century, but thinking well ahead, its owners have already applied for planning permission to extend workings that would gobble up 200 acres inside the Park at Wormhill. The Park Board refused the application on the grounds that it was premature, but a lingering fear remains that economic considerations may eventually result in the ground being literally cut from under the Board's feet.

Even without this additional intrusion, a chunk of the Peak Park, of a size equivalent to a football pitch and the height of a two-storey house, is sliced away every week. What particularly irks the environmentalists is that 70 per cent of the precious stone that is hacked out of the Park goes back underground as hardstone core for roadbuilding. There does not seem much to show by way of compensation for the white dust that disfigures villages like Sparrowpit and Stoney Middleton, the day and night rumble of heavy lorries carrying stone from the quarries to adjacent cities—and all too often carving chunks out of the stone walls bordering roads laid down in the horse and cart era—or the pall of black smoke from the quarries west of the A515; least of all for the sort of ugly blot that disfigures Eldon Hill, making the approach to Sparrowpit from the south or west a horrifying experience. But when quarrymen ask if jobs and the saving of import bills are no recompense you find yourself faced with the old insoluble equation of beauty and hard economics, though the conservationists point out that other, more widely distributed minerals, such as sandstones and gravel can be used as aggregates for roads, though admittedly more expensively.

Outside the Park, the mess is even worse, especially around Buxton and Wirksworth, but a much higher proportion of the limestone goes to the iron and steel and chemical industries which have fewer alternative raw materials. And one source of limestone has at least gone underground, taking with it its ugly, noisy crushing plant. Since 1959 stone has been extracted from a limestone mine—perhaps the only one in Britain—with 5 miles of galleries tunnelling to a depth of 250ft under Middleton Moor, just west of Middleton-by-Wirksworth, to produce high-grade stone used in the manufacture of glass. Its products also serve the sugar industry and go into concrete aggregate in the construction industry, a use, incidentally, for 20 per cent of the stone from within the Park. In limestone mining, if it is practicable elsewhere, there lies a possible compromise that could satisfy both the economists and the conservationists.

Nowadays limestone from the Peak is used in more than twenty different industries, but quarrying for it began locally to serve the needs of builders and farmers at least as early as

Roman times. The Roman bath that was excavated on the site of Buxton Crescent had lime walls, lime mortar, a lime-based-cement wall facing and a floor of a type of concrete made with lime, coarse sand and blood. There is no such clear evidence of its early use in agriculture, but Antony Fitzherbert, a Derbyshire man, writes of lime burning for use on the land in his *Boke of Husbandry* in 1521 with no suggestion that it was in any way a novelty. On some manors from even earlier times, inhabitants had the right to take limestone from certain 'town quarries' as they still have at Eyam. The lime kiln became a familiar sight in the Peak, and fragments of some survive today.

Another early use for lime was in lead smelting, but the large-scale movement of limestone out of the area was impossible before the cutting of the canals and particularly the opening of the Peak Forest Tramway that made Dove Holes an important quarrying centre and enabled Samuel Oldknow to build a battery of 12 lime kilns at Marple producing 2,500 bushels of lime daily in the 1790s. As late as the 1880s some 600 tons of lime and limestone were being dispatched in 30 or 40 narrow boats daily from Buxworth quay. From Buxworth, too, went much of the lime for the mortar used in the building of the Lancashire cotton mills. Meanwhile the opening of the Cromford & High Peak Railway had given an impetus to quarrying developments south of Buxton. The last 30 years of the nineteenth century saw equally rapid development between Millers Dale and Chinley along the Midland line to Manchester. Since then 'the whirligig of time' has played another of its strange tricks. The canals and railways that came into being largely because the roads were inadequate for the movement of large quantities of heavy goods, like stone, have been abandoned in favour of movement by roads which are still inadequate—and unsuitable—for the movement of large quantities of heavy goods.

Fortunately for the economy of the Peak, if not for its appearance, new outlets for limestone in the steel and chemical industries coincided in the 1870s with the collapse of one of its basic markets with the beginning of the great agricultural depression that was to last at least until World War I. Spreading lime as a fertiliser on fields on the limestone uplands may seem as futile as a gift of oil to the Shah of Persia, but paradoxically much of the limestone uplands are deficient in lime. The reason for this apparent absurdity is leaching. This is the process by which soluble salts are washed out of the surface soil and carried down to be redeposited at a lower level. On the top of the limestone plateau at above 900ft, and on moderate slopes, this process occurs, leaving the fields deficient of lime, as is also the case, less surprisingly, on the gritstone.

Despite these deficiencies, agriculture in the Peak is in reasonably good heart, or at least it was until the astronomical rise of animal food prices in the early 1970s. And with all this talk of rocks and minerals it is easy to forget that the Peak District is still predominantly a farming region and that, in the words of the Park Board's *Structure Plan,* 'farming activity has created most of the scenery of the Peak District'. The value of food and other agricultural produce from within the Park reached almost £12 million in 1972.

These products came mainly from small owner-occupied farms. Though there has been a slight trend towards the consolidation of holdings recently, the 'factory farm' is still hardly in sight and the grubbing up of hedges—or their stone equivalents—is almost unknown. About three-quarters of the farms are under 75 acres in size and almost two-thirds under 50 acres; farms of over 250 acres are rare indeed. On the gritstone hill farms it is hard to make a living out of less than 100 acres, and even above that size incomes have to be supplemented by government subsidies and often by a second job in quarrying or catering for tourists. A crop of campers or caravanners is often the most profitable item in the hill-farmer's harvest.

But hill farming on the Dark Peak is more a way of life than a search for riches. Apart from the perks from visitors for some, it is based on sheep and cattle rearing. The stock are grazed on the moorland rough pasture in the spring and summer, while the better land round the farm on the lower slopes or in the valleys is used for growing hay and grazing cattle. In autumn the animals are brought down to lower land; most are sold, the remainder graze the more sheltered land, receiving additional nutriment from hay and silage. The picture that W. H. Hudson saw from Axe Edge some sixty years ago of 'small cottage-like stone farmhouses sprinkled over the earth . . . the meanest-looking, most unhomelike farmhouses you will find in England' would not look very different today, except that there are fewer farms, for those uplands south-west of Buxton have a declining population for reasons as much connected with poor communications as with the poverty of the land. Since Hudson's time more valley pasture there and farther north has been drowned by the reservoirs, while only sheep are allowed to graze in the water-gathering grounds because of the risk of pollution from cattle. But some of the hill farmers who remain may tell you that there are compensations in the way of peace and tranquillity that root them to the spot despite the gales, the 60in of rain and all the other hardships.

Dairy farming is the thing on the White Peak, with some slight recent increase in stock raising. The fields, like the farms, are usually small, but the output of liquid milk large, helped as it has been over the past century by the easier means of distribution offered first by the railways and now-adays by lorries. It is normally sold through the Milk Marketing Board. Friesians and Ayrshires are the most common dairy cattle, but the dual-purpose Shorthorn possibly outnumbers them slightly overall. It is also found crossed with such beef

types as the Hereford and Aberdeen Angus. The increased
need for home-produced meat has seen quite an influx of the
hardy Galloways on the high gritstone country in the north-
east and north-west.

The traditional sheep of the Peak are the speckle-faced,
hornless Derbyshire Gritstone, sturdy, active sheep that stand
up well to bad weather. Once called Dale of Goyt sheep, they
are still numerous on the moors round the head of their
native valley, wandering perilously across the unfenced main
roads between Buxton and Whaley Bridge and Macclesfield
in their search for tit-bits from picnicking motorists. There
was a decline in the popularity of the Gritstone in the 1960s
and there may now be an equal number of the slightly
smaller but equally hardy Swaledale. There are also a few
flocks of Scottish Blackface and Lonk breeds, both horned
sheep. Much rarer are the Whitefaced Woodland, a very
ancient Peakland breed once popular round the Woodlands
Valley, north-east of Edale. At the beginning of World War
II they had been reduced to a single flock, probably because
of their slowness in maturing, but they are now slightly more
numerous. On the lower ground such heavier and more
fastidious breeds as the Kerry Hill and Clun are fairly
popular. The hard winters of 1947 and 1963 took a heavy
toll of Peakland sheep, but the losses have since been made
good.

The southern foothills of the Peak round Ashbourne were
the breeding place of the splendid Shire Horses, which are still
numerous enough round there to have their own classes at
local agricultural shows. The fuel crisis of 1974 prompted
some revival of their use as working horses, but the Texan
and Middle Eastern oil magnates who have recently invested
in Derbyshire Shires probably wanted them as status symbols
rather than to haul ploughs.

The first cheese factory in England was opened at Longford
in that same district in 1870 and still stands, as do others

only slightly later at Reapsmoor, Glutton Bridge near Earl Sterndale, and Grange Mill, but none is now used for cheese making. The only working cheese factory in the Peak is at Hartington, where the Milk Marketing Board took over from a private firm in 1962 and continue a tradition that started in 1900 of producing not Derbyshire cheese, as one might expect, but a high-quality Stilton. More than thirty of the work force of about fifty are women, which not only maintains a long-standing local tradition of women cheese-makers—cheese presses stand unused in most Peak farms—but also provides jobs for women in an area where suitable employment is hard to find, though quite a large number of women are now collected by private buses from a widely scattered area to work in a mushroom farm operating in former RAF buidings at Harpur Hill, near Buxton, and in the valleys of the Derwent and Goyt there are jobs for them in the old-established textile mills.

These mills, though they did not grow naturally out of the rocks, like most Peakland industries, did depend on the fast-flowing streams that came down from those rocks and some still make use of this water, at least as a subsidiary source of power. Some of the early cotton mills are now used for other purposes, mostly for varied light industries which cause no environmental problems and are therefore especially welcome in the Peak. Such industries are comparative new-comers to the area. The only long-established large concern with no obvious geographical link with the area is Ferodo Ltd, who make friction brake linings at Chapel-en-le-Frith. But there is a connection. Herbert Frood, the firm's founder, was a boot salesman who noticed in his travels around the Peak that local carters often tied old boots—possibly made at Stoney Middleton or Eyam, which were then small centres of boot manufacturing—over their wooden brake blocks that wore away easily through friction against steel wheel rims. In a wooden shed in the garden of his home, Rye Flatt,

Combs, using a small water-wheel powered by a tiny stream, he invented in 1897 a brake-lining material made from laminated hair belting impregnated with a bituminous solution. In 1903 he took over the old Sovereign Mill in nearby Chapel-en-le-Frith for the manufacture of what he called 'brake shoes'. In 1920 Ferodo became a public company and later built a 16 acre factory that became the largest single unit producing friction linings in the world. Now part of the Turner & Newall Group, and, incidentally, employing a large number of women as well as men, the firm still preserves at Chapel the original garden shed and uses a tarmacadamed half-mile stretch of the former Peak Forest Tramway near Chapel Milton to test the brakes of high speed cars. The Stodhart tunnel on the same line is used to test the effect of humidity on braking performance.

But perhaps the biggest growth industry in the Peak is tourism. Since the mid-1960s the number of day visitors to the Park has trebled to about 16 million. In addition, the Park Board say, in 1973 visitors stayed 150,000 nights in hotels and guest houses and 635,000 on camp and caravan sites. In all, nearly 17 million visitors spent £9,500,000 that year inside the Park. And when you recall that such popular tourist centres as Buxton and Matlock are outside the Park, you can see that tourism in the Peak is big business indeed.

Alongside these large industries whose turnover is reckoned in millions of pounds, a number of small concerns make a living out of traditional and often ancient crafts. Most surprisingly perhaps in an area where thatched roofs are rare, George Mellor of Cromford finds plenty of work for himself and three assistant thatchers, though most of it lies outside the Peak. Farther to the north-east, on the far side of East Moor at Holymoorside, William R. Walker & Sons still find a market for the besoms they make with birch collected from the Sherwood Forest, while in a splendid old workshop overlooking Tideswell market place W. G. Hun-

Page 157 'The supremely beautiful Snitterton Hall', near Matlock

Page 158 Chatsworth, the west front, with Tudor hunting tower *(top left)* and cascade *(extreme right)*

stone maintains a long family tradition of producing exquis-
itely carved wooden ecclesiastical furniture to beautify not
only Tideswell Church but other churches much farther afield.

Another family concern that has celebrated its centenary
is the Rowsley Corn Mill which still uses water power to
grind barley and maize and to mill flour. The grandfather of
Edward Caudwell, head of what is now E. Caudwell (Rowsley)
Ltd, founded the mill on its present site in 1864. About half
a century ago the original undershot water-wheel was replaced
by the two present turbines which are still powered by a leat
from the river Wye. Milling is now carried out by rollers
instead of the original millstones, but the building itself is
little changed.

The technique of building stone walls has also changed
little over the centuries and still provides full-time employment for a few free-lance craftsmen in the Peak, though there
are slight local variations according to the nature of the
available stones. Two foundation courses, or 'footings', are
sunk into the ground, giving the base of the wall a width
of about 2ft, but the wall tapers to approximately 15in at the
top. The wall is built with two faces, which are bound by
'through stones', usually set at 2ft and 4ft above the footings
to prevent 'bellying out'. Small stones are placed by hand
into the gaps between the faces above and below the 'throughs'.
The weight of the wall binds these 'fillers' together to give
the wall its strength. The coping stones, or 'cap' stones, are
usually held by their own weight, but mortar is occasionally
used here 'to make assurance double sure'. Boundary walls
are usually 5–6ft high, but those merely separating fields may
be lower. 'Cripple holes', or 'creep holes', are sometimes left
low in a wall to allow sheep—but not cattle—to wriggle
through, and stiles through or over the wall are sometimes
built in. By tradition, the amount of work to be covered in a
day was decided by throwing the heaviest hammer and
working to where it fell, but stonewallers say that building

K

a 'rood' of 7yd of wall is a good day's work and in the past they were often paid by the rood.

Ropes were made in the entrance to Peak Cavern, Castleton, for 400 years until the recent retirement of the last rope-maker, Mr Herbert Marrison.

9 THE BUILDINGS

MANY visitors to the Peak go to see the stately homes for which Derbyshire is justly famous. Actually only three of those regularly open to visitors lie within the National Park and only two, Chatsworth and Haddon, are in Derbyshire, Lyme Hall being just over the border at Disley in Cheshire. But these three make up in quality for any shortage in quantity, and in any case other houses such as Kedleston, Hardwick, Sudbury and Oakes-in-Norton are suciently close to the Peak—and certainly handsome and interesting enough—to warrant a visit.

Every summer some quarter of a million visitors go to Chatsworth, which puts it high in the unofficial league table of stately homes that do not go for such gimmicks as lions, funfairs or autograph-signing noblemen. What the visitors go to see is what a French soldier who knew Versailles and Fontainebleau called 'the finest palace in the world', and what since then has been known to every guidebook writer as 'the palace of the Peak', though the present Duchess of Devonshire, who lives there and should know, has called it 'a town'.

A town indeed it is in size with the eleventh Duke of Devonshire and his Duchess as mayor and mayoress presiding over its affairs, entertaining their guests and employing the sort of labour force required to run a small town, including a comptroller, a mole catcher and a team of masons who are, according to the duchess, every bit as good as those who

built the house, which should help to dispel the idea that we
have lost our craftsmanship.

The best way to approach Chatsworth is either from the
moors to the east, across what Defoe called 'a howling wilderness' or from the south along the road from Rowsley. Coming
this latter way, you enter the park over the humpback Beeley
bridge and soon get a first, incomparable view of the house,
which stands on a terrace to the east of the Derwent with its
gardens sloping up behind, gently at first and then steeply
to the woods on the top of the hill where an Elizabethan
gazebo, known locally as 'the hunting tower', peers out above
the treetops. It is a superb view of a superb house.

The present mansion is the second on the site. The first
was built by the redoubtable Bess of Hardwick and her
second husband, Sir William Cavendish, on land which he
had bought in 1549 for £600, a shrewd bargain for a man who
had already been granted a considerable amount of monastic
land by a grateful Henry VIII as a reward for his activity in
arranging the dissolution of numerous monasteries that
had previously owned this land. Building did not begin for
several years and was not far advanced in 1557 when Sir
William died, but it was certainly completed by 1564 when
a contemporary who shared the prevailing dislike of Peak
scenery described it as 'an incomparable jewel in an ignoble
setting'. Bess's mansion conformed to the conventional Tudor
style, being square with square corner towers and central
gatehouse turrets. Virtually nothing remains of that house
in which Mary, Queen of Scots, was kept a prisoner on at
least four occasions in the custody of Bess's fourth husband,
George Talbot, Earl of Shrewsbury, but the ruins of Queen
Mary's Bower, where she took the air, and the gazebo on the
hill have survived from that time.

The fourth Earl of Devonshire built the present house,
almost fortuitously, between 1685 and 1707. When he started
he apparently intended no more than a modernisation of the

original mansion. At that time he was comparatively poor, and out of favour with James II. When he finished, 32 years later, his fortunes were restored and along the way—in 1694 —he had become the first Duke of Devonshire as a reward for his substantial part in helping to put William III on the English throne. Incidentally, the Devonshire in the title was fortuitous too; Duke of Derbyshire was obviously intended, but somebody somewhere wrote illegibly.

The rebuilding was done in two parts. By 1696 the Duke, in between quarrels with his architect, the Dutchman William Talman, had pulled down two fronts of the Elizabethan house and rebuilt them in the Classical style of the period. It was the first great house in England to be built—or partly built— under the contract system. At that stage Talman resigned or was sacked, the workmen—mostly Londoners—were un- doubtedly sacked, and after a few years of contemplating his unsatisfactory hybrid house, the Duke, perhaps inheriting the building urge from his great-great-grandmother, decided to go ahead and finish the house in the Classical style by direct labour; or fairly direct—there were labour troubles, even strikes, when the workmen resented the absence of regular wage packets, which sometimes happened when the Duke had put the money on an unsuccessful runner at Newmarket. ('He hath lost', wrote his agent on one of many occasions, '. . . more than £1,500.') But the house was eventually finished; the Duke died the following year.

Except that the sixth Duke, unwisely but not disastrously, turned Sir Geoffrey Wyatville loose from 1832 to 1842 to add a north wing, the house is outwardly just as the first Duke left it. Internally it is a treasure house of magnificent craftsmanship by such artists in their different media as Laguerre, Verrio, Tijou and Samuel Watson, the latter a lesser-known name than the others because almost all his work was done at Chatsworth. He was a young man from Heanor in east Derbyshire who carved with astonishing

163

versatility and skill in stone, marble and wood. His wood carving was so good that for years it was assumed to have been done by Grinling Gibbons until documentary evidence established the truth. His son Henry founded the marble works at Ashford-in-the-Water in 1748. Some of the marble at Chatsworth came from Holland, but most materials were local; the gritstone from quarries at Beeley Moor and Bakewell Edge, grey marble from Calver and blackstone from Sheldon Moor, making it very much a Derbyshire house.

But for many people the best parts of Chatsworth are the park and gardens, especially perhaps the lake and the Emperor and Sea Horse fountains and the cascade that pours down the slope east of the house. That was not the opinion of the Hon John Byng (later Viscount Torrington) who, visiting the estate in 1789, recorded in his diary that the cascade 'when dry is a disagreeable sight, and not much better when cover'd with the dirty water they lower from the hill', and was determinedly unimpressed by the rest of the grounds and, for that matter, by the house; Hardwick, he thought, was 'worth a dozen Chatsworths'. But then Byng was habitually disgruntled and most visitors are as delighted with Chatsworth as Elizabeth Bennet was with Pemberley, which Jane Austen based on Chatsworth, but there is amongst Derbyshire people a curious sense of partisanship about Chatsworth and Haddon. The anti-Chatsworth brigade say 'it's just a museum', which has certainly not been true since the Duke and Duchess of Devonshire returned to live there in 1959, and the pro-Chatsworth enthusiasts are inclined to dismiss Haddon as 'cold and bare'. I must say I like them both; but they are so totally different they cannot be compared.

Haddon Hall lies just over the hill to the west of Chatsworth, but in atmosphere and architectural style it is centuries away. Haddon was almost complete as it stands today when Bess began to build the first Chatsworth. In 1689 when the rebuilding of Chatsworth had barely begun, Celia Fiennes called Haddon 'a good old house'. It is in fact one of the finest examples of a medieval mansion—with some Tudor additions, including the long gallery, which was almost an afterthought—surviving in Britain.

Haddon owes its preservation to neglect. Unlike most country mansions that have been modernised and 'improved' to catch every wind of changing fashion, it was left to look after itself throughout the eighteenth and nineteenth centuries and so evaded the grasp of the Georgian improvers who would have turned it into an attractive but utterly different Palladian mansion and the Victorians who would have pulled down the original medieval battlements and towers and substituted imitation, romanticised battlements and towers. Byng was almost correct when he wrote in 1789 of 'this poor abandon'd place' being 'totally deserted . . . and uninhabited', but Edward King, who saw it seven years earlier, was more perceptive if more wordy in hoping 'that this princely habitation may never come so far into favour as to be modernized, lest the traces of ancient times and manners, which are now so rarely preserved in this country anywhere, should be so utterly lost here also'. His hopes were realised.

The history of the house can be quickly told because in a sense it has no history. It has been owned by only four families and has never changed hands by purchase. William Peverel, one of the illegitimate sons of William the Conqueror, held the manor at the time of Domesday, but a later Peverel backed the losing side in one of the civil wars of the next century and forfeited his estates in 1153. Haddon passed to a sub-tenant, William Avenel, who left it in 1170 to his daughter who had married Richard Vernon, and the house belonged to the Vernons for the next four centuries, passing in 1567 to the Manners family when Dorothy Vernon married John Manners. (Serious historians wince at the suggestion of an elopement, but it is an attractively romantic story that fits snugly into the Haddon ambience, and there is really no evidence either way.) Anyway, Haddon still belongs to the Manners family, Dukes of Rutland.

Most of what you see today at Haddon was built by the Vernons and Manners, though the Peverel Tower and parts of the chapel were already there by 1170. Richard Vernon obtained a licence from Prince (later King) John in 1195 to build a 12ft wall round the house. This wall still stands, but the battlements are a sham added in the fourteenth century, a piece of nostalgia for the 'good old days' when such defences were necessary. After Peverel's time, in fact, the owners of Haddon kept out of violent politics, which is another reason why the place is so well preserved. Having built his wall, Richard Vernon was content to leave well alone and it was not until about 1370 that a descendant became restive and put in the present impressive banqueting hall, with its minstrels' gallery—often filled by musicians at Christmas time and other festive occasions, the Stewards' Accounts tell us—and the kitchen. After that each generation of Vernons, enriched by lead-mining profits as well as by rising land prices, added or altered something, and the Manners at first kept up the pace. Sir John altered the south front and the superb long gallery to their present form about 1600 and his son altered and reroofed the chapel.

That was virtually the end of the building history of Haddon. After Sir John's grandson became first Earl of Rutland in 1641 the family transferred their resources to another family house, Belvoir Castle in Leicestershire. In 1702, the year before the Earl became the first Duke of Rutland, the family made Belvoir their principal seat, leaving 'the bat and the owl . . . the only inmates' of Haddon's 'remaining splendour', as Rhodes put it in his *Peak Scenery* in 1819.

That the splendour has remained is due mainly to the ninth Duke of Rutland, father of the present duke. He found, early in this century, that the house, although never entirely neglected, whatever Byng and others had said, was in poor shape. In 1910 he began a most thorough restoration that lasted until 1932. And it really was a restoration. Almost every stone, every piece of timber was examined and if possible put back. The banqueting hall was reroofed and a few stones replaced, otherwise hardly anything is less than 350 years old in what the usually restrained Sir Nikolaus Pevsner so aptly called 'the large, safe, grey, lovable house of knights and their ladies, the unreasonable dream-castle of those who think of the Middle Ages as a time of chivalry and valour and noble feelings'.

Lyme Park lies well away from Chatsworth and Haddon, more than 1,200ft above sea level on the western edge of the Peak, but historically and architecturally it occupies the middle ground between them. It has an Elizabethan kernel inside a Palladian shell. The Legh family, who acquired the estate in 1347 and handed it over to the National Trust exactly 600 years later, pulled down the medieval mansion in the sixteenth century and replaced it with a suitably trendy new house with all the latest status symbols, such as chimneys, glass and a long gallery. Then, about 1720, a later generation decided it was time for a change to something grander to grace an estate that was 9 miles in circumference and something that was more in keeping with the times. So they called in the fashionable architect Giacomo Leoni, who had been brought over to England by the Palladio-worshipping Earl of Burlington, to design a new south front in the Palladian style without too much interference with the interior. The result is a most impressive façade, though perhaps, as Ralph Dutton suggested in *The English Country House,* one not entirely in sympathy with its surroundings, and a most charming partly Tudor interior—long gallery and all. Today the councils of Greater Manchester and Stockport jointly lease house and estate from the National Trust.

'If the Italians', wrote Dutton, with Leoni and perhaps Lyme in mind, 'could build palaces for princes, it was the supreme talent of the English architects that their houses supplied fitting accommodation for country gentlemen.' There are many manor houses in the Peak to illustrate this point. Their architects are often not known, or have names that mean little today; their houses are usually unpretentious, plain and not excessively large, but they look exactly right in their setting, mainly because they were built of local stone and for occupation rather than admiration.

It follows that these houses are not, nor ever have been, open to the public in the conventional sense, but at least five are open to some of the public. The house that Arkwright built at Cromford and called Willersley Castle—and Byng, who saw it nearing completion in 1791, called 'an effort of inconvenient ill taste'—is now a Methodist guest house. North Lees Hall, Hathersage, the Thornfield Hall of *Jane Eyre*, a fifteenth-century small manor house, is a privately run guest house. It stands on an estate of 1,280 acres that ranges from moorland bog, through gritstone edge, bracken and heather moor down to mixed and conifer woodland and improved pasture land. All this and the house were acquired by the Park Board in 1971, the year after the purchase of Losehill Hall, Castleton, a Victorian mansion that the Board opened in 1972 as the first residential study centre run by a National Park in Britain. As a house, Losehill may be less exciting than some, but its courses, all related to the environment in general and the Peak in particular, are amongst the most exciting things happening in the area in the 1970s. There are excellent facilities for field studies, too, at Ilam and Hartington, both youth hostels. Ilam Hall is not the mansion that Dr Johnson visited, but its Gothic-Revival successor built for a shipping magnate named Watts-Russell early in the nineteenth century, though the setting that Johnson admired is unchanged. Hartington Hall is more typical of Derbyshire, an E-shaped limestone manor house built in 1611—though in style it could be fifty years earlier—and enlarged in Victorian times. It has a panelled room in which Bonnie Prince Charlie reputedly slept, but if all the traditions about Charlie are true his brief, ill-starred visit to Derbyshire must have been something of a whistle-stop tour.

If there is such a thing as a typical Peakland house, it stands, like so many of the villages, on an often narrow shelf on a hillside—sometimes as high as 800ft, as at Castern, above the Manifold—with a steep rise behind the house to act as an effective windbreak. Sometimes the back of the house seems to be built almost into the hillside, as at Hassop and Parwich, both fine Georgian houses. Parwich Hall is a rarity, a red-brick house in a limestone village, which must have been a fairly determined and costly piece of what Stephen Potter called 'one-upmanship' on the part of Sir Richard Levinge, who built it in 1747. However blatant it may have looked then, the brick has mellowed since and the house now blends surprisingly well into its surroundings, as does Great Longstone Hall, also built of brick in that same year.

Another interesting feature of Parwich is that it sits close to—if slightly above—the village centre rather than aloofly in a park at a more discreet distance as later eighteenth- and nineteenth-century houses tended to do. This endearing mateyness is also evident at Tissington (built around 1610), Eyam, Hopton, Winster and the supremely charming Snitterton, amongst others, and even more so at Youlgreave, Cartledge and Taddington, where the halls are little more than enlarged versions of the farmhouses and cottages in the village streets.

This is no disparagement; Youlgreave and Cartledge, especially, are outstandingly fine examples of the smaller manor houses, but an acknowledgement of the worth of the less conspicuous homes of the yeomen and artisans. Documentary information about individual houses of this

169

type is rare. For houses more than about a century old even the original building date is often a matter of guesswork. But just occasionally some evidence comes to light. We know, because he kept a rather spasmodic diary, that Leonard Wheatcroft, parish clerk, school teacher, tailor and general factotum of Ashover, began to demolish a house that stood 'on my owne ground' in 'a place which I now call by the name Hockley' in July or August 1671 in order to build a house of his own. Using very direct labour—his own entirely it seems—he completed it some five years later, though unfortunately he failed to record the exact date of completion. But there it stands today, at Hockley in Ashover parish, a pleasant little stone cottage with a steeply pitched roof and a single chimney stack and the little garden rising sharply up the hillside behind in the typical Peakland manner. And under the eaves in the front of the house is a stone bearing his initials and those of his wife Elizabeth and the date 1676.

Skilful detective work by members of the Bakewell and District Historical Society and others has brought to light a great deal of information about what is now called the Old House Museum at Bakewell. It was built as a parsonage in the fifteenth century and was used for that purpose until 1549 when the Dean and Chapter of Lichfield sold it to Ralph Gell of Hopton Hall. In 1778 the Gells leased the Old House to Richard Arkwright, whose son bought it in 1796. The Arkwrights converted the house into six 'dwelling units', to use the modern jargon, and the barn next door into four more, but eventually sold the house and land to the Duke of Devonshire. He disposed of the land in 1861 and then sold the house to the local workhouse master, who did rather nicely for himself by living in one house and letting the others, an example followed by later owners until the last ones, the Harrison family, gave it to the Society in memory of their parents. The last tenant left in 1967, some five centuries after the first one moved in. Since 1967 the Society, having managed to effect the substitution of a preservation order for a demolition order, have been working hard to remove the Arkwright alterations and restore the house to its sixteenth-century condition, making, as happens when working on very old houses, some interesting accidental discoveries on the way.

The house in 1549, according to Dr J. Marshall Jenkins, who has studied it carefully, was roughly T-shaped. The leg of the T, running north and south, had the house-place (a sitting-room/kitchen)—and possibly a dairy and certainly a passage from porch to staircase—on the ground floor and two chambers, one with a fireplace, above. This wing measured roughly 40ft by 20ft. The cross wing, some 34ft by 20ft, had parlour and buttery on the ground floor and the principal bedchamber and a small chamber above. Over the small chamber was a loft, possibly used as a servant's bedroom.

It is worth giving space to this detail because as Dr Jenkins says, 'the plan is typical of yeomen houses built in Derbyshire and Yorkshire during the fifteenth, sixteenth and early seventeenth centuries. It stems from the convenience of placing accommodation on two levels across the end of a medieval hall of two-storey height.' I know of no other house of this kind in the Peak which has been studied so carefully, but Cartledge Hall, a mile or two to the east of the National Park, would repay similar research. The house is reputed to have been built in 1492, the year when Columbus was trying to convince his sceptical sailors that their voyage across the Atlantic would not necessarily end in their slipping over the edge of the world. The house-place, still the main living room, was probably originally the only living room. The five bedrooms are reached up four separate staircases—of stone except where badly worn stone has been replaced by timber—leading directly out of the house-place. The parlour, with its 120 oak panels, was added between 1560 and 1610 during

171

the period of extensive rebuilding that lasted, nationally and locally, to about 1640.

Like so many Peakland houses, Cartledge lost its status as a small manor house after the Civil War and in 1857 it was described as 'an ancient farmhouse'. Eighteen years later one of the several bedrooms with magnificently moulded ceilings—a notable feature of many houses close to Sheffield —had become 'a roosting place for fowls'. By 1947 it was, in the eyes of local officialdom, unfit for habitation. But, as at the Old House, Bakewell, the demolition men were thwarted, this time by one local man, Basil Doncaster, who bought the house and restored it to its former glory.

Thus Cartledge, though a most unusual house, has a history that follows a fairly familiar Peakland pattern. Many such houses were built or extended between 1560 and 1640, quite often by families who had no obvious link with the area. Some of these houses subsequently slipped a rung or two in the social ladder and became working farmhouses. Such declines generally occurred either immediately after the Civil War because, as at Cartledge, its owner had backed the wrong side or, during the period 1873–1939, as a result of the agricultural depression or rising taxes, including death duties. Since World War II, however, large sums of money have been spent on restoring such houses, the cash coming either from increased profits from agriculture, or, more often perhaps, being brought in by new owners with flourishing business interests in Sheffield or other large towns just outside the Peak. One may grumble cynically about these refugees from the profitable messes they have helped to create, but it would be unfair not to acknowledge that without them many a fine Peakland house would have gone for ever.

Similarly a great many small farmhouses and village cottages have been 'tarted up' during this same period. Again, it is all too easy to be sentimental or superior about this. Some mistakes have been made, of course, but generally these houses have become better places to live in without losing much of their external attractiveness. Fortunately the summit of the great twentieth-century rebuilding period came after 1951 by which time the Peak Park planners were around to prevent such solecisms as the use of red brick for walls and dark Welsh slate for roofs in an area which calls for walls in varying shades of grey with gritstone tiles—or some suitable modern substitute—for roofing. Only on the approaches to the Park has there been some dubious development, and fortunately, so far, not too much of that. Some of the credit for this must go to Gerald Graham Haythornthwaite, an architect and town planner, who as technical adviser since 1945 to the flourishing Sheffield and Peak District Branch of what is now the Council for the Protection of Rural England and a member of the Peak Park Board since 1951, has been a most alert watchdog able invariably to bark—and when necessary to bite—at the first approach of ugly development in and around the Park.

Although stone has been the accepted building material in the Peak for at least four centuries, remains of timber-framed construction have increasingly come to light in recent years, as at the Green Hall, Ashbourne—admittedly on the very edge of the stone belt—and in many cottages. Indeed it has been suggested, on the slightly negative evidence that cottages earlier than the fifteenth century are rare, that timber-framed houses were numerous before the 'Great Rebuilding'. That may be so, but nowadays you have to search hard for outward signs of timber construction; stone predominates; limestone in limestone areas, gritstone in the gritstone country, or both in villages like Hartington which have both stones to choose from. But it is not quite as simple as that. In the limestone areas gritstone, which as I have said is a more pliant stone, is often used for quoins, lintels, window sills and coping stones, and even in the gritstone areas limestone—often from Hopton Wood—is sometimes used for doorsteps. Walls may be of ashlar—finely dressed, smoothly finished stonework; coursed, where the stones are laid, like brickwork, in courses; or rubble, where the stone is in different shapes and sizes giving an irregular effect. Windows with stone mullions are still quite common; some have transoms too, but pointed, sham-Gothic windows are not uncommon, especially in areas where some early-nineteenth-century landowners were anxious to keep abreast of contemporary trends.

Most Derbyshire villages have cottages worth a second glance. If I suggest that Winster, Hartington and Eyam have more than most, somebody is bound to come up with three other villages that are at least equally rewarding. To pick out individual cottages as especially worthy of note is even more dangerous, but I would suggest the row of six seventeenth-century Plague Cottages at Eyam and the Old School House at Hartington as being good examples of 'typical' Peakland houses. The Old School House at Hartington bears the date 1721, but that might be a rebuilding date; like so many local houses it seems ageless and has probably seen many piecemeal alterations. Built of limestone, it has gritstone quoins, lintels, sills and mullions, with small leaded panes in some windows; it is an excellent example of the way the two stones can blend attractively. However, a typical Peakland house is difficult to classify for there are subtle variations in building from one village to another. In the north the houses belong more to the Pennines than just to the Peak, and there are considerable variations between houses on the eastern and western fringes of the area as influences have crept in from outside. But having said that, you have to agree that there is at least a clearly recognisable family likeness. Parachuted down from an aircraft anywhere in the area where two or three houses were clustered together, you would know you were in the Peak.

The same cannot be said of the churches. There is little

Page 175 Two types of building stone at Hartington. The walls are of limestone, gateposts, lintels and mounting block of gritstone

Page 176 Old Glossop, showing seventeenth-century houses

of the homogeneity that you find, for example, in the great Marshland churches round King's Lynn or the magnificent towers of Somerset, probably because there was never a period of outstanding and uniform prosperity in the Peak. But this is not to say there are no fine churches; there are. Tideswell, for one, would be outstanding anywhere. From whichever direction you approach, you get an early anticipatory thrill at the sight of the eight-pinnacled tower rising high above the squat buildings of the little town that straggles across a low, sheltered bowl to the surrounding rim of hills. Closer inspection confirms that first favourable impression. The church is very beautiful and very large: 'probably', says a leaflet inside—characteristically in an area that has considerable respect for records—'the largest in Great Britain today at an altitude of 1,000 feet above sea-level'. This, I can neither deny or confirm, but I should guess there are few more impressive or satisfying at even lower altitudes. It is lofty, airy, contains much good woodwork—some medieval and some by a Victorian, Advent Hunstone—is rich in pre-Reformation monuments in brass and stone and still contrives to remain uncluttered. But from the point of view of the architectural historian, the most interesting thing about Tideswell is that it was built—or at least rebuilt on the site of a smaller church—over a period of about fifty years in the fourteenth century, with a brief interruption caused by the Black Death in 1348–9. By then chancel, nave, aisles and transepts were finished. After the break the chancel was apparently considered inadequate and was replaced by the present one that has so rightly been described as 'massive and grand and dignified'. By 1400 the tower had been built. Since then there have been no major alterations to the main fabric.

In a sense, then, Tideswell church is a curious survival like Haddon Hall, and for rather similar reasons. In the fourteenth century the little town was prospering as a market and lead-mining centre. In the nineteenth century, when architects and enthusiastic clerics were finding there was nothing half so much worth doing as simply messing about with churches, prosperity had gone and so the church remained gloriously untouched. And inside you can see today how architectural tastes changed as the church progressed. It starts off in the Decorated style; then there is an indeterminate bit, and finally the tower completely in the Perpendicular style.

Most of the other Peakland churches have bits and pieces to show from most centuries, including the nineteenth. Alstonfield, for one, has retained its box-pews from the seventeenth century—including the squire's pew in which Charles Cotton sat. Hartington escaped lightly and sits grandly on a slope above the houses, as does Bakewell, which has retained a little Norman work and some magnificent alabaster tombs, including one of Dorothy Vernon and her husband and a much earlier one of Sir George Foljambe (died 1377) and his wife, which Pevsner calls 'an internationally remarkable monument'.

Peak District churches are fairly rich in monuments in alabaster, which usually came from quarries at Chellaston, now a southern suburb of Derby, or from Tutbury, only a little further away in east Staffordshire. Youlgreave, a thoroughly rewarding church, has some good examples, as does Ashbourne, though the monument that catches the eye there is Thomas Banks' white marble figure of Penelope Boothby (died 1791), with a most moving inscription: 'She was in form and intellect most exquisite. The unfortunate Parents ventured their all on this frail Bark, And the wreck was total.'

There is a particularly fine alabaster tomb-chest with effigies in the picturesque and most interesting church at Ashover. It is to Thomas Babington (died 1518) and his wife. Some of Ashover's fascinating memorial tablets are on a different level of poignancy from Penelope Boothby's at Ashbourne. After reading the inscription to Francis Parkes, who 'by his Natural

Genius and great Industry Became a wonderful Proficient in ye Politer Art of Painting', and numbered among his virtues 'Singular Modesty, Sweet Disposition, Strict Sobriety, Ingenious Conversation, Unusual Diligence, Uncommon Skill', it is something of a relief to turn to the tablet to John Milnes, a local lead-mine owner, who was damned with faint praise in an astringent 'N.B. T'was said he was an honest man.' More endearing is the tablet to the 'Memory of David Wall, whose superior Performance on the Bassoon endeared him to an extensive musical acquaintance . . . His social life closed on the 4th of December, 1796, in his 57th year'. But perhaps the most remarkable thing in the church is the list of rectors back to 1086. There were only eight of them between 1621 and 1942; all but one Bournes or their descendants, Bourne Nodders. Joseph Nodder held the living from 1835 to 1878; his son, John Bourne Nodder then continued in office until his retirement in 1942. There were then no more Nodders in Orders to take over this family living.

That Ashover, in a lead-mining district, should have a Norman lead font may not sound particularly surprising. There are, after all, some thirty lead fonts in the country. But what is surprising is that this is the only one in Derbyshire.

Almost certainly the oldest and most interesting Christian relic in any Peakland church is the sculptured stone slab now built into the wall of the north aisle at Wirksworth. It is a coffin lid, found over a grave containing a skeleton below the chancel in 1820. Experts agree that its elaborate carvings show a strong Eastern influence, and it now seems to be accepted that it came from the sarcophagus of an early Celtic missionary of the second half of the seventh century.

Wirksworth, Ashbourne and Bakewell are all ambitious town churches with interestingly contrasted spires. Ashbourne's is 212ft high, but its effect is rather lost from a distance because of its position in a deep bowl. Wirksworth's, on the other hand, is a strange little lead cone on an impressive tower. Bakewell's spire, built about 1340 but taken down and rebuilt five centuries later, is the most conspicuous because of its dominating position, whereas Wirksworth Church is tucked away behind a semi-circle of old houses in what is virtually a charming minor close. Ashbourne stands some little way out of the town centre at the end of what is undoubtedly the finest street architecturally in all Derbyshire and is best seen in spring when the spacious churchyard is a riot of daffodils.

Of other notable Peak churches, there is space only to mention two. St John's, Saltersford, known locally as Jenkin Chapel, was built in the style of the local small farmhouses in 1733 and has remained unchanged; box pews, reading desk and all. The tiny hamlet of Hassop has a large, severe Classical-Revival Roman Catholic church, built in 1816, that seems to have strayed from some fashionable London square and looks as out of place in the Peak as a stockbroker dressed for the City on Kinder Scout.

Church and inn often sit close together, so close that in one village, which had better remain nameless, the organist used to slip out for a quick pint during the sermon. There is that sort of juxtaposition at Ashover, where an incription on the Crispin Inn proclaims that 'This house probably dates from the year 1416 when Thomas Babington of Dethick and several men of Asher returned from the Battle of Agincourt, which was fought on St Crispin's Day'. An unlikely story, but there is truth in another inscription on this old posting house telling that 'In 1646 Job Wall, landlord of this inn, withstood the King's Troops in the doorway and told them that they should have no more drink in his house as they had had too much already, but they turned him out and set watch at the door till the ale was drunk or wasted'.

Unfortunately, what the nineteenth century did—with some honourable exceptions—to the churches in the name of improvement, the twentieth century has done even more damagingly—again with some honourable exceptions—to the inns. Too many have become smart eating houses with gin and tonic bar trades, and not all modernisation schemes have been carried out as tastefully as Lt-Col Haythornthwaite's sensitive improvements at the Barrel Inn, Bretton, built in 1637 more than 1,300ft above sea level. Happily, many inns—usually off the beaten track—have managed to retain their old character and most are more willing to serve a sandwich with their beer than would have been the case even twenty years ago. To attempt to name them would be to invite unwelcome development and be utterly unfair, since I have not sampled every Peakland pub. So I must confine myself to a few that have particular architectural merit or some other special claim for a mention, like those two that are nationally famous because of their remoteness: the Snake and the Cat and Fiddle which is reputedly the second highest sited inn in England.

Even then selection is impossibly hard; so many inns in the Peak have retained their good looks, outwardly at least. The Peacock at Rowsley, for instance, looks a typical Derbyshire manor house of the best local period, and that, roughly, is what it was. It was built by John Stevenson, agent to Grace, Lady Manners, and his name and the date, 1652, are still over the door. By 1876, when James Croston stayed there while writing *On Foot in the Peak,* it had become 'the far-famed Peacock at Rowsley, a comfortable roadside inn—the beau idéal of an old English country hostelry'. In 1973, as one of only 98 country hotels in Britain to receive the British Tourist Authority's special commendation, its reputation remained high, especially among anglers. The peacock is the emblem of the Manners family, which explains why another Peacock inn—at Baslow—having now been acquired by Chatsworth Estates, has been transformed into the Cavendish Snake.

If one could spend a pleasant but perhaps heady week

touring the inns of the Peak, one could spend at least several days visiting the industrial buildings, many of which bear no resemblance to Blake's 'dark satanic mills'. The valleys of the Derwent and its tributaries have some splendid examples. Cromford has some of Arkwright's earliest mills, zealously watched over by the Arkwright Society, who have a museum and information centre in an old corn mill. Arkwright's original mill is still in use, though now as a colour works. There is still some doubt about which building in the complex came first, but all were erected before 1800, though the cast-iron aqueduct carrying water across the road from Cromford Sough and Bonsall Brook to drive the mill's over-shot water wheel was built in 1821 to replace an earlier wooden one that superseded the original leat about 1785. The water from the lead-mine sough was always warm, ensuring that the machinery never stopped even in times of severe frost. There is something rather forbidding, fortress-like, about the early mill, but the Masson Mill, a little farther north along the A6 on the edge of Matlock, is much more cheerful, almost flamboyant. Built in 1783, it hints at Ark-wright's growing confidence that accompanied increasing prosperity reflected in a six-storey building in uncharacteristic red brick with Venetian windows and a jaunty cupola.

More austere, but solid and dignified, is Calver Mill, an 1805 rebuilding of an eighteenth-century cotton mill destroyed by fire. It is now the headquarters of an old-established Sheffield firm making stainless-steel sinks who have achieved a successful blending of modern buildings with the old mill. But of all the old cotton mills, perhaps Cressbrook (see Chapter 6) is the most satisfying both architecturally and in its setting.

Not all the Peakland mills were concerned with the cotton industry. The woollen trade from the east and silk manufacture from the west spread out into the hills and valleys of the Peak in the eighteenth and nineteenth centuries and the remnants of these trades within the national park have been well described by Helen Harris, but there is one building that must be mentioned here. It is the main surviving relic in Wildboarclough of the mid-eighteenth century when the little village became a silk-manufacturing centre. Three mills were built, one of which had machinery installed by James Brindley. These mills have now gone—the last, containing Brindley's machinery, as late as 1958 on the eve of the birth of conservation. All that remains, apart from the former agents' house, is the imposing administrative block, which is now the village post office. It must surely be the biggest and most impressive village post office in Britain.

TOWNS AND VILLAGES

THREE places have strong claims to be considered the capital of the Peak: Bakewell, administrative centre of the Peak Park Joint Planning Board, Matlock, the administrative centre—though not strictly the county town— of Derbyshire, including much of the Peak outside the Park, and Buxton, the main tourist centre. My choice goes narrowly to Bakewell if only to follow the slightly dubious precedent set by earlier writers who tended to call it 'the metropolis of the Peak', and through sheer personal prejudice. It seems to me to be a splendid place to live in; highly attractive, friendly, and, with just over 4,000 inhabitants, small enough for one to know almost everyone and big enough to avoid any one might not happen to like. Even the disgruntled John Byng found it grudgingly, 'a much better place than I had expected'. A century earlier Celia Fiennes had thought it 'a pretty neate market town', and the comment, if not the spelling or punctuation, would pass muster today.

Bakewell is an old settlement. The Anglo-Saxons, as usual, chose their site carefully at a point where the Wye was starting to widen its flood-plain after passing through the limestone plateau but could still be comfortably crossed by tracks descending from the sheltering hills. The ancient parish, though basically on limestone, contained a deep bed of shale that provided excellent pastureland and there was gritstone close at hand. Above all, there was a good supply of drinking water from Baddecan Well, a place name that had been corrupted to Badequelle when Domesday Book was compiled. To command the river crossing, Edward the Elder built a castle in 924. Its mound stands close by the site of the former railway station, which is now, ironically, a rather less conspicuous historical relic. Fragments of Anglo-Saxon work remaining in the fabric of the church suggest that the original building was at least as early as the castle. In 1086 it was the only Peakland church with two priests, surely a necessity in a parish covering an area extending from Buxton to Beeley.

Bakewell became a market town in 1330 and has retained its character as an agricultural centre ever since. Monday, market day, is always an enthralling day in Bakewell for anyone with a taste for country life, but the great day of the year is the Thursday in the first complete week in August, the day of Bakewell Agricultural Show, the 'little Royal', which claims to be the largest one-day show in England. Bakewell Show is held on the Meadows, a delightful—if sometimes muddy—riverside setting whose peace is periodically threatened by rumours of an impending bypass.

Apart from the show, the town is famous for its Bakewell puddings—not tarts, please, even if they look like tarts. The very first one was made—fortuitously—by the cook employed by a Mrs Greaves who kept the Rutland Arms in the town centre. It was in this inn that the cook one day mistakenly put jam at the bottom of a pudding case and the filling at the top instead of in the reverse order. The pudding had an unusual dark top, but was voted a hit by the guests and became a regular feature of the menu. When the cook made her will with the help of a local schoolmaster-turned-auctioneer named Radford, she wrote out the recipe and left it to him. He passed it on to a Mr Bloomer, whose family have used it ever since. There is no secret about its ingredients: just eggs, butter, jam, flaky pastry and a spot of almond essence, but the actual mixture is a closely guarded family secret.

The Park Planning Board has its headquarters a little way

out of the town at Aldern House on the Baslow road, but has an excellent information centre strategically placed in Bridge Street not far from the Rutland Arms in one of the most interesting of the town's numerous older buildings that have survived the pompous 'improvements' of the nineteenth century and the road widenings of the twentieth century. These buildings are well documented in a *Town Perambulation* by A. L. Knighton, one of several useful duplicated booklets published by the Bakewell & District Historical Society. Among the most interesting of Bakewell's buildings is Bath House, built in 1697 by the Duke of Rutland in an attempt to jump on the spa wagon that was gathering momentum at that time. But Bakewell was unlucky. Its chalybeate water was colder than at Buxton, which was already an established resort, or at Matlock, which opened its bath in 1698. Bakewell has preserved its bath, but ceased to be a spa long ago.

Buxton has a curious riches to rags and back to riches history. After the Romans left, its importance declined. Domesday Book gives it merely a passing reference as Buchestanes, and not until 1811 did it acquire a parish church, after William Wilberforce had pointedly compared the facilities for worship with those for revelry. A small chapel or shrine dedicated to St Anne, the patron saint of the principal well, had, however, been built about 1200 to cater for the halt and the lame who came to the holy well and left behind their discarded crutches and other offerings. In due course Henry VIII's commissioner, Sir William Bassett, of Meynell Langley, put a stop to such 'idolatry and superstition' by taking away 'crutches, shirts and shifts which was offered . . . and locked up and sealed the baths and wells at Buxton that none shall enter to wash there till your Lordship's pleasure be known'. His Lordship was Thomas Cromwell, whose pleasure was probably to have the chapel demolished. No trace of it remains, the present towerless, aisleless St Anne's Chapel having been built on a fresh site in 1625. It is Buxton's oldest surviving place of worship.

The third phase in Buxton's rise to spadom began not long after Bassett's visit, when George Talbot, Earl of Shrewsbury, built what was virtually an hotel—though it came to be known as the Old Hall—on the site of the present Old Hall Hotel. The earl's Old Hall was four storeys high, with among other amenities, 'a great chambre and other goodly lodgings to the number of thirty', according to a Dr Jones, a Derby physician, whose treatise *Buckstones Bathes Benefyte,* published in 1572, was a highly effective piece of sales literature that deserves an honoured place in the history of holiday brochures. It attracted such noble visitors to Buxton as the Earl of Leicester and Lord Burleigh, but Mary, Queen of Scots' visits undoubtedly owed less to Dr Jones than to her jailer, the Earl of Shrewsbury. Mary visited Buxton four times between 1573 and 1582 in search of health, though the earl suspected her, the first time anyway, of malingering, and Queen Elizabeth I worried about security. Each time, Mary spent several weeks at the Old Hall at some expense and inconvenience to the earl, who would have preferred to remain at Chatsworth. On one visit she scratched on a window with her ring the words:

> Buxton, whose fame thy milkwarm waters tell,
> Whom I perhaps shall see no more, farewell.

The Old Hall was rebuilt in 1670, but Celia Fiennes, staying there for two nights 'sore against our wills' seventeen years later found it 'not very good' and the beer 'so bad that very little can be dranke'. 'Sometimes', she complained, with some justification, 'they are so crowded that three must lye in a bed.'

It was to improve such conditions and to make Buxton a serious rival to Bath as a popular spa that the fifth Duke of Devonshire launched in 1780 one of the finest and most ambitious of eighteenth-century planning schemes. With John Carr of York as his architect, he spent £120,000 on building the Crescent, which has been described recently as 'the finest building of its kind in England', though Byng, who admitted his dislike of modern buildings, called it 'a labor'd quarry above ground', and 'a huge Mausoleum'. Obviously modelled on the larger and more famous Royal Crescent that John Wood had erected at Bath, it suffers in comparison because it had to be built in a hollow owing to the refusal of another landowner to sell a more commanding site that the duke coveted. Nevertheless, it was an extraordinarily bold venture in a town that then had a resident population of little more than 600, and it remains, unarguably, one of the finest Georgian town buildings in northern England. Built of local stone, much of it quarried on the site, it contained, when it was completed in 1784, three hotels, all with private access to the adjacent baths, a magnificent assembly room with a richly decorated ceiling that has happily survived, and numerous shops. Just to the north, the duke and Carr built superb stables surrounding a circular exercising yard today enclosed under a large iron dome, on the site of what is now the Devonshire Royal Hospital.

These improvements reduced the grumbles about accommodation but not those about the problems of reaching Buxton. This inaccessibility accounts for the slow growth of the resort, despite such further developments as the laying out of Duke's Drive (1795), the Cliff Gardens and the Italianate parish church of St John the Baptist; the church, and probably the gardens, designed by Sir Jeffrey Wyatville. But transport inadequacies had the merit—in the eyes of those who braved them—of keeping the place 'select', though by halfway through the nineteenth century there were mutterings amongst the aristocracy of the growing number of self-made Lancashire businessmen and their wives who were arriving to take the waters.

The coming of the railways in 1867 opened the floodgates. The Palace Hotel was built close to the stations in 1868, the Pavilion Gardens laid out about the same time and the Pavilion itself added in 1871 in the bright and breezy, iron and glass seaside pier style of the period, followed by the Opera House just after the turn of the century. The resident population grew from 1,877 in 1861 to 6,021 in 1881. Buxton as a flourishing Victorian spa had arrived, but, as tends to happen in such cases, the aristocracy had departed.

The heyday of spas ended with World War II. Buxton's thermal baths are closed, but you can swim in the healing water in the new swimming pool which Princess Anne opened in 1972 and you can still drink the water by the glassful at St Anne's Well, now contained in a small enclosure which it shares with the Information Centre opposite the Crescent. The Crescent has been restored by the Derbyshire County Council and now houses a fine library and council offices. The outward appearance of Buxton has changed little, but its style as a resort has undergone some subtle alterations. It is perhaps more of a base camp than the summit of the mountain, though it has the only theatre in the Peak, a cinema, concerts and other entertainments for those who prefer—or are compelled —to spend a sedentary holiday rather than use the town as a centre for exploring the Peak. With a population of around 20,000, Buxton is also what estate agents describe as 'a much sought after residential area', still linked to Manchester by a good commuter rail service, and it is, as passing lorries tend to remind you, an important administrative centre of the limestone quarrying industry, as well as the main shopping centre of a considerable area and—though this is hard to comprehend when you look down into Buxton's leafy bowl from the surrounding hills—Britain's second highest market town.

Matlock is a second Buxton, with salt and vinegar added. It is a spa—more correctly now a resort—with a shorter, less

aristocratic history than Buxton's, lacking the noble patronage
and the architectural merit, as well as the inhibitions of its
rival, but making up for it by the grandeur of its setting that
John Wesley found 'pleasant beyond expression'. Nathaniel
Hawthorne had 'never seen anywhere else such exquisite
scenery as surrounds this village of Matlock', by which he
probably meant Matlock Bath, then in its heyday as a spa,
possibly unaware of the seven other Matlocks, which, with
eight more hamlets now form a town of about 18,000 people
that should correctly be 'The Matlocks' but is more usually
covered by the generic name of Matlock.

Scenically, it must be the most beautiful town in the
Peak. Much of it lies in a deep gorge of the Derwent, a little
reminiscent of the famous Wye gorge between Monmouth and
Chepstow. The A6 shares the narrow valley floor with the
river, forcing the railway to tunnel through the almost sheer
limestone cliffs on the east bank. The buildings crowd along
the roadside or climb steeply up the slopes of Masson on
the west, where one man's front door opens almost on to his
neighbour's rooftop. At the northern end of the gorge, where
the road swings right to cross the medieval bridge, the sides
of the valley are less precipitous; and on the east bank, town
streets with revealing names like Bank Road and Steep Turnpike climb stiffly upwards on gradients of 1 in 6 or 7.

If you drive up one of these streets and then work back
southwards along the ridge towards Old Matlock, Starkholmes
and Riber—or better still, park your car and go carefully
on foot to the edge of High Tor—you may agree with
Prebendary Gilpin that 'it is impossible to view such scenes
without feeling the imagination take fire'. Peering down into
the gorge, 400ft below, or above it beyond Masson and the
Heights of Abraham to the seemingly unending Peak hills
you could feel with him that 'every object is sublime and
wonderful'. Descent into the gorge at a high-summer weekend
may bring reservations. It is wiser to go in spring or autumn

when the crowds and the commercialism are less obtrusive.

That commercialism crept in gradually after the discovery in 1698 of a thermal water spring at what is now Matlock Bath. The earlier history of the Matlocks is obscure. Domesday Book records that 'Meslack' was a berewick of the royal manor of Metesford (almost certainly Matlock Bridge), which had a lead mine, 8 acres of meadow and some woodland, but was otherwise 'waste', and it had little else of note—except for the lead mines whose disused workings are the caverns now shown to tourists—until that momentous discovery in 1698.

Even then prosperity came slowly. Defoe, some twenty-five years later, found that the spring had been 'made into a very convenient bath, with a house built over it'; but Matlock was far from being a rival to the established spas. He correctly attributed this to two causes: 'namely a base, stony, mountainous road to it, and no good accommodation when you are there', though he heard of an intention to 'build a good house to entertain persons of quality, or such who would spend their money in it'.

This intention was carried out in the 1730s with the erection of 'two commodious buildings connected with the bath', which became, after the findings of other springs, the Old Bath Hotel. About the same time a coach road was built from the bath along the southern part of the gorge to join the hilly east-west road at Cromford, and improvements were made to the rocky bridlepath to Matlock Bridge.

These changes encouraged enough visitors to justify the employment of a 'neat Orchestra furnished with a harpsichord and diverse other instruments' in the Assembly Rooms at the Old Bath Hotel, where half a century later a youthful, love-sick Byron endured hours of jealousy watching the unresponsive Mary Chaworth dancing with other partners. Dr Richard Russell, who did for Matlock what Dr Jones had done earlier for Buxton, drew attention to the orchestra, also remarking on the 'Politeness of the Company and the easiness of the Charges', which amounted to 3 shillings (15p) a day for meals with free lodgings and bathing. By the end of the eighteenth century, prices in the three good hotels were still reasonable at 5 shillings (25p) a week for a bedroom, though bathing now cost 6 pence (2½p). But politeness was declining, according to Byng, who reported peevishly that 'by new buildings, and an increase of lodging-houses, the quiet and society of the place is lost, and it begins to become noisy, and divided into parties'.

There were good reasons for this growth. Not only was Matlock Bath sharing the increasing popularity of the English spas but its scenery struck exactly the right romantic note that the spirit of the age demanded. The Rev Richard Warner was probably right in saying in 1802, that 'the larger number of visitors . . . consisted of admirers of its beauties rather than drinkers of its waters'. And for those who tired of both beauty and the waters there were, in addition to the usual attractions of a spa, the shops where ornaments were made from the local fluorspar and Blue John, and the petrifying wells.

Despite such attractions, Matlock Bath remained a select resort, offering 'gaiety without disputation, activity without noise' even after the cutting of what is now the A6 opened a way for daily coach services from Manchester, Nottingham and Derby. But its character changed with the arrival of the railway. Opened in 1849 with great rejoicing (and free ale at the Old Bath Hotel), it brought Matlock Bath within reach of the day tripper from Derby and Nottingham. No longer intimidated by high coach fares, or by a change from train to canal boat at Ambergate and a tiring walk from the canal head at Cromford, they poured in their thousands out of the gay, Swiss-chalet style station at Matlock Bath to find the exploiters, the Victorian 'wide-boys', waiting to greet them and relieve them of their surplus cash. We complain a great deal nowadays about modern commercialism and nobody could say that modern Matlock is entirely free from it, but it is mild compared with what went on in the second half of the nineteenth century and to a reduced extent in the first half of the twentieth century. Victorian visitors to Matlock seem to be agreed that it was then impossible to walk ten yards down the main road of Matlock Bath without being cajoled, bullied or even seized by men eager that they should enjoy such experiences as viewing the caves or the petrifying wells, boating on the river or even having their photographs taken.

The effect of this blatant commercialism was to drive away those 'persons of quality' who preferred to take their pleasures more quietly. Some of these refugees did not go far to find what they sought. At the northern end of the gorge, high above the railway, a new resort was springing up at Matlock Bank that had much to offer them. Matlock Bank owed its growth virtually to one man, John Smedley, a rich, eccentric industrialist. Having, by the middle of the nineteenth century, re-established a failing family hosiery business at Lea Mills, close to Florence Nightingale's home at Lea Hurst, he found a fresh outlet for his unflagging energy in the newly fashionable science of hydropathy. Convinced that his own health had been restored by hydropathic treatment, he saw water as a panacea. He contrived to get himself appointed as unpaid —and unqualified—medical adviser to the first hydro at Matlock Bank, and within two years had bought the place.

Smedley's Hydro was immediately successful. Victorian England, it seemed, was full of hypochondriacs, willing to pay two guineas a week to live austerely in gracious surroundings for their health's sake. Some two thousand of them yearly were soon finding their way to Smedley's, and expansion became necessary.

Gradually there grew up the enormous, indigestible block of dark gritstone that still dominates the other buildings of Matlock Bank like a battleship surrounded by motor launches.

It was designed by Smedley himself, never inhibited by self-doubts about his own all-round competence.

He certainly managed the Hydro successfully, by giving his patrons just what he wanted. His rules were numerous and strict. Visitors began their day at six o'clock with a compulsory plunge into cold water and ended it precisely at ten at night. In between, they ate simple but ample meals, drank nothing alcoholic and were forbidden to hear any but sacred music—for Smedley was something of a religious fanatic. For breaking rules they paid fines on a sliding scale ranging from one penny for lateness at meals to half a guinea for entering a lady's bedsitting-room. But they survived this rigidly organised regime and returned repeatedly for more.

Rival establishments sprang up, and Matlock Bank flowed downhill to merge with the growing shopping centre at Matlock Bridge, forming the modern town, which looks today like a piece of deliberate—and rather unimaginative—town planning. You feel that the hillside setting demanded something more exciting than the too-regular grid pattern, which is much less interesting than the enforced haphazardness of Matlock Bath. And the local gritstone—mostly from nearby Bentley Brook quarry—strikes a chilling note, especially when translated into municipal Gothic public buildings. A public building is what Smedley's Hydro has become. It survived on a declining scale as a hydro until 1955, when Derbyshire County Council bought it and moved its administrative offices there from Derby. This injected new life into the town so that today—with Matlock Bath still a holiday resort—there is no decayed spa atmosphere about the place. Recent developments, such as the road widening in Matlock Bath that opened up the river front and deservedly won a Civic Award, have brought genuine improvements to a town that has had the wit to realise that its river is a considerable asset.

To appreciate Matlock fully, you must see it from above;

from Black Rocks at Cromford, perhaps, for a superb long view; or better still from Riber, where another of John Smedley's memorials— a fantastic sham-Gothic castle—broods over the town from a wildly unsuitable hilltop site, 800ft up. Originally, as the last of many philanthropic gestures that included the building of schools and chapels, he intended to build an observatory. But the site was wrong, and what emerged—six years before his death in 1874—was this absurd castle whose inconveniences his widow loyally endured until her own death eighteen years later. Since then, after serving as a school and a food ministry's store it stood derelict until the British Fauna Reserve bought it from the Matlock Urban Council for £500.

Ashbourne, only about ten miles south-west of Matlock, is utterly different in character. It is one of those solidly satisfying characterful market towns that have remained small enough to escape the acquisitive eyes of developers through-out the ages. As the 'gateway to Dovedale' it naturally becomes congested but rarely jammed with traffic at week-ends in summer; otherwise except on market days—Thursdays and Saturdays—when its attractive, cobbled, hillside market place is 'fair thronged', as they say locally, it is quietly distin-guished but utterly unpretentious. After rapid growth in the early Middle Ages, when its population seems to have approached 2,500 by the fourteenth century, it has taken the next six centuries to double that figure, putting it marginally ahead of Bakewell in population. Its now growing number of light industries, mostly springing from agricultural ante-cedents, are tucked away unobtrusively and there are more good buildings of most periods from the sixteenth century onwards—mainly in Church Street and St John's Street—than in any other town in the Peak.

The most handsome of these, apart from the parish church which George Eliot called 'the most beautiful mere parish church in England', is the original grammar school building of 1586, but the most famous is The Mansion, an early eighteenth-century house almost immediately opposite, where Dr Johnson often used to stay with his old school friend Dr John Taylor. Close by are several good groups of almshouses, dating from the seventeenth and eighteenth centuries. At the other end of the town, what is left of Ashbourne Hall, where Bonnie Prince Charlie slept on his advance to, and retreat from, Derby, is now used as a library and offices.

Between Ashbourne and Matlock is Wirksworth, the 'Snowfield' of George Eliot's *Adam Bede,* another place that has grown only slightly since Defoe called it 'a large well-frequented market town' so that 'large' is hardly the adjective that springs to mind today. Since Defoe saw it in its lead-mining heyday, Wirksworth seems to have dozed for two and a half centuries, waking only recently to find itself not only a quarrying centre but a small town of considerable character with a central core of handsome urban buildings—mainly of the eighteenth century—that seemed to be crumbling away through neglect. The last few years have seen a great transformation. Derbyshire County Council, whose planners have now a good eye for townscapes, has designated the town centre a conservation area, thirty buildings have been listed, and a newly formed Civic Society is carrying out a general improvement scheme.

Something of the same sort might be done for Chapel-en-le-Frith, a dark-grey, villagey little town that has lost its 'frith' but not its picturesque hillside position nor a few good but slightly fading buildings. Most of these buildings cluster round the cobbled market place that retains its stocks and market cross. Close by, on the site of the foresters' chapel, is the fine church, mainly of the fourteenth century, but with eighteenth-century alterations, and box pews from the early nineteenth century. But even more than a restoration of its buildings, Chapel needs a bypass. Its steep main street, which happens to be the main A6, is a nightmare for motorists who

196

find themselves in a convoy of stone-bearing lorries. But a bypass would need sensitive planning to avoid marring a lovely landscape dominated by such fine hills as Chinley Churn (1,480ft) to the north and Eccles Pike (1,213ft) to the west.

New Mills is an Industrial Revolution product straight off an L. S. Lowry canvas. It is usually ignored by topographical writers, but it has a certain rather weird attraction for me, largely because of the unevenness of its streets, especially perhaps Union Road, which crosses the deep gorge of the Goyt on a high sloping viaduct not far from the confluence with the Sett. New Mills has one other advantage over some of the Lancashire cotton towns that it closely resembles; it is easy to escape from into beautiful surroundings.

Much the same might be said of Glossop, but that would be a superficial view; it is a much older, larger and altogether more interesting place. In fact it is really two places. Old Glossop ('Glott's Valley') was the centre of an ancient, scattered parish that in medieval times was 16 miles long and 5 miles wide. It has retained much of its village character in an area round the market cross and parish church, with an especially fine group of seventeenth-century mullion-windowed, gabled cottages in Church Street. Modern Glossop was a planned town of the 1820s and 30s. From about 1810 cotton mills had been springing up along the valley of the Glossop Brook, encouraged by the principal local landowner, the Duke of Norfolk. With the opening of the Snake Pass road in 1821, the hamlet of Howard Town became a potentially important crossroads site. The duke, seizing his chance, had a new town laid out with public buildings, places of worship, water supplies, a town hall in Norfolk Square in 1838, and a market in 1845, the same year in which the branch railway arrived. The subsequent history of Glossop is closely related to that of the Lancashire cotton industry to which it was linked. The boom town of the nineteenth century declined in prosperity and population towards the middle of the present century, but with greater diversification of its industries its population has recovered to more than 24,000, making it the largest Peakland town. In 1970, both Old Glossop and the duke's Norfolk Square area became conservation areas.

The prosperity that came to Glossop quite late in its history bypassed certain other ancient Peakland market towns which eventually lost their status, but fortunately not their charm. Hartington and Longnor, for instance, cannot muster 1,000 inhabitants between them, but both retain such vestiges of their urban past as spacious market places overlooked by dignified nineteenth-century market halls, now used for other purposes, good inns, shops and rather more than you would expect of the professional services, for both places are still focal points for hinterlands of scattered farms and tiny villages with declining populations. Only a century ago, James Croston described Hartington as 'an old-fashioned and somewhat important country town', and if you substitute 'tourist centre' for 'country town' his description would stand today, as would his comment that 'it is thoroughly Derbyshire in appearance', though it is within half a mile of the Staffordshire boundary. It is certainly busy at weekends in summer, but its population has increased little since Croston's time and the market that received its original charter in 1203—earlier than any other in Derbyshire outside the county town itself—petered out within living memory, though annual October sheep sales still attract farmers and onlookers from a wide area.

East of either Longnor or Hartington, the nearest shop is about seven miles away at Monyash, which ceased long ago to be either a market or lead-mining centre and is now un-mistakably a village, though a handsome one with a green and mere softening the austerity of the stone cottages. Farther north, Tideswell looks more like a town and though its population is declining it still has more people than have Longnor,

Hartington and Monyash combined. But apart from the splendid church, and adjacent eighteenth-century George Inn with its pleasing Venetian windows, it is rather short of good buildings and other tourist attractions.

Castleton, on the other hand, is obviously doing very nicely indeed as a tourist centre. Its narrow streets are often choked by cars and coaches, despite a sensibly spacious and relatively unobtrusive car park, and by ramblers heading for the surrounding, inviting hills and amblers making for the caves and the ruined castle that dominates the place, but there is a peaceful, village quality about the area round the church and on the green behind it. Though Castleton's tourist trade has been long established, its population is only about a hundred more than in the mid-nineteenth century after the local lead mines failed.

Winster's population has only just crept back to the 753 that it had reached in the first census return of 1801 before a lead-mining boom carried it over the 1,000 mark in 1841. In those days it supported five or six pubs. Today the only survivor—the significantly named 'Miner's Standard'—is outside the village on the main road. But 'village' is really the wrong title for Winster. It still wears the look of a town and has a delightful little seventeenth-century market hall, owned by the National Trust, to strengthen that impression. The other buildings in the long main street and in the huddle of narrow alleyways—'jitties' or 'ginnals' in the Peak—that climb up the hill to the south, Cornish-fashion, may not individually be worth driving twenty miles to see, but collectively they are a delight. And there always seems to be something cheerful and surprising happening in Winster; Morris dancing in the main street, a pancake race on Shrove Tuesday, a band playing, or the annual Wakes. On my last visit, I encountered a Polish wedding; the real thing—bride and groom in an open landau, following a band in the national costume. Yet, somehow, Winster is missed by the tourists, probably because it is hidden from the main road by a fold in the hills, although it is now just beginning to be found by commuters.

Ashover is already something of a dormitory village for refugees from Chesterfield, Clay Cross and other places along the eastern Coal Measures, but fortunately has lost none of its rugged charm or slightly eccentric atmosphere. It has always been a place of character and characters. Set in the Amber Valley against a background of trees and steep hillsides (its name means 'ash tree slope'), it was once a lead mining 'Liberty' outside the King's Field, and a market town until 1829. It is now, rightly, a conservation area, with many of its nineteen listed buildings grouped together in the shadow of its dominant church spire. But outside the core of the village are numerous scattered settlements with names like Milltown, Hackney, and Eastwood, whose Old Hall was ruined by parliamentary soldiers in 1646. Some sixty years later Eastwood acquired a spa house, but in 1767 this became a poorhouse, a nicely ironic ending to a truly riches to rags story. The oddest-named settlement is 'The Rattle', an aural reminder of the days when the cottagers worked at their stocking-making machines.

Crich, another large, hilly, straggling village with an urban past, still has a three-storey stockingers' cottage with long windows on the upper storey, a relic of this trade that once found work for the womenfolk of the lead miners and quarrymen on the eastern side of the Peak. But today most Crich people work either in Ambergate or in the nearby small industrial towns of the coalfield.

From the story of these former market towns, now amongst the most attractive of Peakland villages, an economic pattern emerges. In general, population densities have varied according to the state of the local industries, particularly lead mining. Just a few more examples from nineteenth-century census returns will make that clear. The 25 per cent rise in Sheldon's population in the 1850s is explained in the 1861 returns 'by the employment of lead miners from Cornwall'; the halving of the population of Wensley and Snitterton around that time was due to there being 'fewer workmen in the lead mines'; and the drop of one-third at Foolow between 1811 and 1851 was attributed tersely to the 'failure of a lead mine'. Towards the end of the nineteenth century there was a general decline over the whole of the Peak except in the larger towns, especially the north-western 'boom towns'. On the eastern side the lost ground has been more than recovered, mainly owing to the development of motoring and the subsequent influx of commuters. In central Peakland communities are now fairly static or even declining, which is a more pronounced feature in the south-west. At Sheen, between Longnor and Hartington, the population dropped from 331 in 1931 to 241 in 1971. In that sort of area a vicious circle turns. Quarries close, less labour is required on farms, so people move out in search of work. Public transport becomes uneconomic and is reduced or ceases to exist, so more people move to the towns, leaving village primary schools to become uneconomic to run. They are then closed and people move in search of education for their children. So it goes on.

From these harsh economic realities, the squirearchal villages are spared. There a carefully planned economy has always been practised, and such villages are also aesthetically amongst the most pleasing in the Peak. Tissington would surely top any opinon poll as the most beautiful Peakland village. Reached only by three lanes, one of which crosses a ford of brake-drum depth, as I once discovered to my cost, it is a picture-postcard village, clustered round hall, church, mere and greens without trace of litter or apparently a blade of grass out of place. Clearly the Fitzherberts, who have presided over the place from the present house since 1611 had heard of conservation long before the word became fashionable. Perhaps they overdid it a bit, keeping the local pub at rather more than arm's length on the main road over half a mile from the village and beyond the lodge and cattle grid that guard the main approach—down a lime avenue—to what is very much an estate village. Thus the place seems to lack life and movement, except during the well-dressing season in the ten days from Ascension Day, when it has too much of both for comfort. But it is certainly at all other times a restful, beautiful spot, and whoever designed the early-nineteenth-century houses to blend so harmoniously with their seventeenth- and eighteenth-century neighbours did a magnificent job.

Ilam was less fortunate. There, Jesse Watts-Russell did a hatchet job on the old village in the 1830s, replacing the old buildings with what Professor Tarn has aptly described as 'some phoney picturesque cottages', erecting an equally phoney Victorian Gothic cross and using more money than taste on 'restoring' the church, though he spared the Saxon font with its carvings thought to illustrate scenes from the life of St Bertram, who is buried under the south chapel. But there are compensations: there is a good family group monument by Chantrey in the mausoleum that was added is 1884, and the setting of thickly wooded hills could hardly be more delightful.

Edensor is even phonier than Ilam, but more successful, to my mind. This is the village that the sixth Duke of Devonshire had re-erected outside the gates of Chatsworth Park to replace the earlier buildings that marred his view. The concept for the layout of the new village probably came from Joseph Paxton, who designed his own Barbrook House just up the Baslow road. But the Edensor houses, apart from Wyatville's Buxton Lodge, were designed by John Robertson in a wide variety of styles from many countries and many periods. No two houses are alike. Not all are equally successful, but the general effect is eccentrically pleasing and the houses were a good deal pleasanter to live in than those they replaced. Apart from one cottage inside the park, whose owner reputedly refused to sell, the only survivor of the earlier Edensor is the Edensor Inn, now the Chatsworth Institute, which was newly built and kept by 'a very jolly landlord' when Boswell visited it in 1775.

Developments at Chatsworth in the late eighteenth and early nineteenth centuries led to the extension of Baslow, a tourist village, now divided, like Gaul, into three parts. The original village grew up round the church and bridge at what is now Bridge End. Far End was a distinct agricultural community on the Sheffield road. Nether End grew up at the edge of Chatsworth Park, and when the Chesterfield road was diverted through the park in 1826, hotels were built here to accommodate visitors to Chatsworth.

Of the other Peakland villages, there is space only to mention four. Eyam seems hardly to have altered in appearance since the plague years of 1665–6 when more than two-thirds of its inhabitants died. Hathersage—the Morton of *Jane Eyre*—despite recent development, is still attractive and has Little John's grave in its churchyard. Rowarth is a tiny gritstone village, tucked away in the hills above New Mills, but well worth seeking out for its good vernacular architecture, as is Alstonfield for its good buildings and charming little greens. But every Peakland village has something good to offer.

11 PEAK PEOPLE

F EW writers have spoken kindly of Peakland people, and some have been decidedly caustic. Defoe considered them to be 'of a strange turbulent, quarrelsome temper', though he was writing chiefly about the lead miners, whose working conditions were hardly conducive to urbanity. The inhabitants of early-eighteenth-century Wirksworth, again mainly miners, were 'rude, boorish kind of people'. Both accusations may have had validity at the time. Certainly disputes in and concerning lead mines were numerous and heated, even violent, but it is equally true that this admirable London-born journalist just failed to communicate with Derbyshire people because he could not understand the local dialect. Indeed he admits as much. Only with the aid of an interpreter was he able to grasp the name of a miner he met near Brassington. 'Nor indeed could we understand the man's discourse so as to make out a whole sentence; and yet the man was pretty free with his tongue too.'

Defoe's difficulty can be appreciated. Even today, after fifty years of radio and half that of television a stranger may be forgiven if he does not immediately understand that 'A inna in; a's wockin in t'Stores at Waser', means simply that 'He is not at home; he is working in the Co-operative Society's shop at Wirksworth'. It may take a stranger a little while to appreciate that when a Peak District farmer talks of 'grains' he means 'greens', and when he speaks of 'green' he means 'grain'. It can be quite confusing.

It is a strange dialect, a cross between Lancashire and

Yorkshire, with more than a dash of the East Midlands thrown in. This is a simplification, of course. The dialect changes almost from one village to the next. The change is not always obvious, but you feel that Professor Higgins would have had no difficulty in distinguishing a Flagg man from one from Flash.

It is a dialect that has retained Shakespeare's 'a' for 'he'. and the pure Anglo-Saxon 'sirrah', which may turn up as 'surra', 'sorry', or 'surrey', and is a form of address like the East Anglian 'bor' and should not be confused with the local 'sithe', which means 'do you understand?'. In fact a man from Shakespeare's time—or even from Chaucer's—would probably find the dialect a good deal more comprehensible than would a modern visitor brought up on a strict diet of pure standard English—whatever that may be. He would certainly agree with the Peakrill that it is perfectly possible to starve with cold, the word being derived from the Anglo-Saxon 'steorfan', to die, and he would be able to cope with 'nesh', which can be synonymous with 'mardy', timid or tearful or may simply mean susceptible to cold or fear. He would doubtless find himself perfectly at home with the short 'a' sounds and the long, heavy 'u' which is almost indistinguishable from the 'o'. There are few sounds more impressive than a Peakland housewife telling a neighbour that she has just bought some wonderful butter, but it defies phonetic transcription.

Peakland folk are rather proud of their dialect and are not hurt when it makes strangers smile. They even enjoy jokes like the one told by Crichton Porteous of the young teacher from the town in her first day in a Peakland village school. Having eaten her picnic lunch, she looked round the playground for somewhere to dispose of the wrapping paper. 'Where's the bin?' she asked a boy. 'Ah've bin 'om, of course', said the boy, 'weer does t'think ah've bin?'

Picnic lunches and school playgrounds have almost gone in these days of spacious refectories in comprehensive glass and concrete palaces with their own playing fields, but the dialect remains—diluted perhaps by the influence of these schools and the BBC—and it is likely to wither only slowly because, like the people who speak it, it has deep roots.

This is one thing that may strike you about the Peak District, especially if you happen to live in one of those large transit camps called Coventry, Derby or Leicester. In 1851 more than half the people of Derby were born outside Derbyshire. In the Peak, away from its eastern fringe and despite the to and fro-ing of lead-mining families, most families have lived thereabouts for many generations.

This is demonstrably true of such landed families as the Vernons, Fitzherberts, Gells, Bagshawes and others who had been around for several centuries before the Cavendishes came to Chatsworth a little over 400 years ago. No Debrett or Burke traces the lineage of less exalted folk, but gravestones and parish registers, if they do not fully chronicle 'the annals of the poor', at least hint that Deans have farmed at Kirk Ireton since Tudor times and that families like the Shimwells, Grattons and many others have lived on the White Peak for at least as long.

It is for this reason that so many old customs survive in the Peak. Well-dressing is the one that attracts most attention, rightly because it is a genuine folk-art that belongs almost exclusively to Derbyshire. In most of the fifteen or so places—almost all on the White Peak—where it is still practised it is a real survival rather than an attempt to cash in on the renewed interest in folklore and 'God wottery'. Attempts have been made to put a date to the foundation of the custom at Tissington; 1348–9 when the purity of the water is supposed to have given the villagers immunity from the Black Death and 1615 when the springs continued to flow throughout a drought that lasted from late March to early August have both been suggested. But almost certainly well-dressing goes back much earlier to pagan times when early man propitiated the gods who would keep the springs flowing on the parched limestone uplands, and paid their insurance premium in wild flowers and other natural objects. Today the villagers make elaborate and skilful designs, usually depicting some religious theme.

Of this and other customs, such as Clipping the Church, which is carried out at Wirksworth on the Sunday following 8 September, and Garland Day at Castleton on 29 May, I have already written fairly fully in my *Old English Customs* and there is no need to repeat myself here. But the survival of the Ashbourne Shrovetide football game through the streets of the little town should be mentioned if only to refute a remark by W. H. Hudson that Peakrills were 'not a happy-looking or a lively people'. Hudson could not have seen Ashbourne with its shop windows boarded up and a wild mêlée in progress for the ball—or to work off ancient grudges —in the little Henmore brook on Shrove Tuesday or Ash Wednesday. He would have thought them lively enough on those days, as he would if he had been able to visit the High Peak Harriers annual point-to-point races at Flagg, or the sheepdog trials at such places as Hope and Ilam. And here again you can see something of the continuity, as well as the liveliness, of Peakland life, because the breeding and training of sheepdogs is something of a family tradition, going back a long way in such families as the Priestleys. Elliots and Ollerenshaws to mention just a few names among those whose skill with dogs is phenomenal. The sort of dedication and concentration that a man requires to make his dogs obey every whistle and almost anticipate his thoughts may partly account for Hudson's belief that Peak people were 'so wholly absorbed in their own affairs and oblivious of the world outside; mentally isolated like the inhabitants of a lonely island'.

The people Hudson met were chiefly farmers and their families, and there may be some truth in his comments. Many Peakland farms are fairly isolated, and in the days before the average farmer had a motor car, the farmer and his family must to some extent have been 'islands unto themselves'. Even today in a small hamlet like Ible, perched above the Via Gellia valley, one must tend to live a self-contained, withdrawn life. Certainly Peaklanders tend to be quiet and reserved, avoiding any display of emotion and not easily moved to laughter or tears. A certain Peakland doctor says that no true son of the Peak ever admits to being in good health. 'Middling' is the most exuberant response one is likely to receive to an enquiry about a person's health. On the other hand, a dying man will admit no more than that he is 'only just middling'. The Peaklander is a moderate man with an intense suspicion of exaggeration.

You can understand what Hudson meant when he found the young people 'too serious—they were even solemn, and gave one the impression that they had all been recently converted to Methodism and were afraid to smile or to say an unnecessary word'. So they had been recently converted—a century or so is recently enough in the Peak. These people gave John Wesley a rough passage in the Peak, as they had earlier done to the Rev William Bagshawe (1628–1702) a native of Litton who is remembered as 'Apostle of the Peak', but when they were converted, either by Bagshawe or Wesley, they stayed converted. The chapels may not dominate their villages like those fortresses of God that the Welsh put up everywhere in the last twenty years of the nineteenth century, but they are there all right and so, even today, is the Nonconformist conscience. The political liberalism that usually goes with it occasionally asserts itself, as it did in 1918 when a Matlock cobbler named Charles White, standing as a Liberal, defeated the Cavendish nominee in West Derbyshire, normally a safe Tory seat, and again in 1944 when Charles White's son, standing for Labour, defeated the Marquis of Hartington. This liberal-nonconformity is less evident in the High Peak constituency, which almost invariably votes Tory.

A later member of the Bagshawe family, squarson of Wormhill, when passing through Peak Forest village one Sunday in 1794, 'was sorry to observe a party of boys playing football'. He spoke to them, 'but was laughed at, and on my departure one of the boys gave the ball a wonderful kick—a proof this of the degeneracy of human nature'. It would be interesting— but almost certainly foolish—to attempt to prove that the influence of this tight-lipped Bagshawe and others of his kind has been responsible for the comparative scarcity of first-class footballers and cricketers who learnt their game in the Peak. But a much more likely reason is the difficulty of finding good pitches for both games in fields that either slope like colliery pit-banks or have been churned up by mineral workings. Potential batsmen are not encouraged to play strokes when they are more concerned with saving their skins, especially, as was the case at Middleton-by-Wirksworth some thirty years ago, when confronted by an opening pair of pace bowlers named Killer and Death.

There are exceptions, of course, particularly in the valleys of the north-west and the east, where both the grounds and the standard of cricket are better. Darley Dale's ground was recognised as sufficiently good to be allocated a John Player league county match in 1975, and for a number of seasons Derbyshire have played one or two games a season on the delightfully rural ground at Buxton, where Grin Low (1,450ft) surmounted by a folly tower known as Solomon's Temple rises up behind the bowler's arm at one end. On a fine day there are few more attractive county grounds in England, and certainly there is no higher one, nor one where cricket is so often interrupted by rain.

Hudson might have argued that apart from Ashbourne football, the Peak has no traditional local outdoor activities like the fell-racing, hound trailing or wrestling of the Lake District, but against that the villagers of Sheen could justly claim that their village tug-of-war team has built up a national reputation in an unusual branch of athletics.

On the whole, though, it must be admitted, the Peak is renowned for sport rather than games, for shooting and fishing at least, if not for fox-hunting; for that you have to go down to the grasslands of south Derbyshire that are part of the Shires. But there is hare-hunting. The limestone and shale country between Buxton and Bakewell has been described as 'Utopian hare country'. It is hunted by the High Peak Harriers, 'the most celebrated pack of harriers in central England', founded as the Stanton Harriers by Mr Pole-Thornhill in 1848, whose kennels have been at the Shutts, Bakewell, since 1901. The pack meets twice a week in the season, and the riders may jump some 150 or so stone walls, blissfully free from wire, in a single day's sport, though it is doubtful if they slaughter the 1,000 hares in 1,234 days, which was the boast of Robert Nesfield, a Victorian Master who was then agent to the Duke of Rutland's 30,000 acre Derbyshire estates.

The hunting field tends to breed eccentrics. The Peak has produced several. One was Florence Nightingale's great-uncle, 'known throughout Derbyshire', says Cecil Woodham-Smith, 'as mad Peter Nightingale'. He was 'a dare-devil horseman, a rider in midnight steeplechases, a layer of wagers, given to hard drinking and low company'. Captain John White was another of those larger than life-sized extroverts who flourished in the early nineteenth century, living in the saddle and usually dying when they left it in attempting some impossible jump. White died peacefully in his bed, but some years earlier the *Manchester Guardian* had reported his death after a nasty fall at Newmarket, a report which White emphatically denied in a telegram to his wife advising her not 'to remarry yet'. White, who once rode 264 miles in a day, built a cock pit at Park Hall, Hayfield, planted a vast number of trees, and typically devoted far more attention to the architecture of his stables—that are now four charming houses—than to his mansion.

These men had none of that solemnity that Hudson noted.

Nor indeed did Charles Cotton (1630–87), who inherited from his father not only Beresford Hall but also a mass of debts that were the result of an over lively life. Cotton never managed to lose his debts or his infectious happiness. His verse may not have been outstandingly good; he may even have been 'coarse and vulgar', as I have seen suggested recently, but not even his creditors spoke harshly of him nor could even Hudson have accused him of being too serious.

One wonders what Peakland people made of Cotton's way of nearly earning a living. Folk scraping a meagre livelihood out of the thin soil, or even more painfully below it, have always tended to regard writing as at best 'a soft option' and not real work at all, or at worst, just plain 'soft', which is just about as hard a word as they use. They certainly underrated the admirable, locally-set and now almost forgotten novels of Robert Murray Gilchrist (1868–1917), who lived for a time at Cartledge Hall, though they read avidly the 132 exciting racing novels of Nat Gould (1857–1922), who began his working life on a Peakland farm and is buried at Ashbourne. But the old Philistinism is passing and there is more respect now for such modern writers as L. Du Garde Peach, who ran his own highly regarded theatre at Great Hucklow until 1971, Crichton Porteous of Two Dales and Alison Uttley, once of Castletop Farm, Cromford, who used her home ground as the location of that classic children's novel *A Traveller in Time* and for much more of her work.

Less than two miles from Mrs Uttley's home there stood, until it was swept away in recent road widening, Glenorchy House, Matlock Bath, where George Newnes, son of a Congregational minister, was born in 1851. Although his sole success as a writer was a school literary prize, he could be called the father of modern periodical journalism. He was a business man who in a flash of inspiration conceived the idea of a weekly paper containing tit-bits of interesting information to appeal to the newly literate products of compulsory education. Unable to obtain from conventional sources the £500 capital he required to launch the paper, he raised the money himself by opening a vegetarian restaurant in Manchester and then selling it for a handsome profit. *Tit-Bits* first appeared in 1881 and still flourishes today little changed except perhaps that the emphasis in the title may have moved from the second syllable to the first. One of his employees was C. Arthur Pearson, who later founded the Cowdray empire, a contributor was Alfred Harmsworth, who went on to launch the *Daily Mail,* and with it modern daily journalism, and to become Lord Northcliffe. Some of Northcliffe's famous advertising gimmicks may have owed their inspiration to Newnes, who initiated competitions for large prizes and free insurance for regular readers in building up his own publishing empire whose richest possessions included the *Strand Magazine,* which introduced Sherlock Holmes and a puzzled Dr Watson to a delighted public, *Wide World,* where 'truth was stranger than fiction' and *Country Life.*

Perhaps Newnes was as near to being a Great Man as the Peak has produced, Thomas Hobbes and Sir Joseph Paxton presumably not qualifying through being born outside the region, though both spent more than half their lives within it at Chatsworth as, respectively, tutor and head-gardener-cum-Admirable Crichton to the Cavendish family. Both George Vernon of Haddon and Dr John Taylor of Ashbourne were regarded by their contemporaries as great men, but Vernon, once 'King of the Peak', is remembered now mainly as Dorothy's father, though there is still a lingering folk-memory of his brand of instant justice that was not above the immediate hanging of a thief caught in the act. Taylor, 'King of Ashbourne' in his time, is now recalled chiefly as Samuel Johnson's friend whose habits were 'by no means sufficiently clerical' and in whose head ran livings and preferments 'as if he were in want with twenty children' instead of being immensely rich. Strangely, he was never vicar of Ashbourne, where he lived and worshipped.

James Brindley was a genuinely great man who, despite his lack of formal education or command of English, fathered our canal system. It may lend weight to Hudson's argument about Peakrills not being 'lively people' that they let 123 years pass after his death in 1772 before they gave him any sort of memorial. This belated recognition took the form of an ornate stone structure over a well on the village green at Wormhill bearing the legend '1895 In Memory of JAMES BRINDLEY, Civil Engineer, Born in this Parish A.D. 1716'. The actual birthplace at Tunstead, a mile away, had to be demolished in Brindley's lifetime because an ash tree forced its way through the cottage floor. That tree in turn was blown down in a gale some years ago, but the Derbyshire Archaeological Society recently planted a sapling on the spot with a plaque nearby to mark the birthplace. The Brindley Mill at Leek which he built in 1752 was restored by voluntary labour in 1974 and is now open to the public on Sunday afternoons and some Saturdays. Just outside the Peak, interesting examples of Brindley's work survive on the Trent and Mersey, Bridgewater and Chesterfield Canals.

Brindley moved back from the Peak to be nearer to his work; two other eminent engineers moved into it to be further away from theirs, in the fashion of the nineteenth and twentieth centuries. Sir Joseph Whitworth (1803–87), armament manufacturer and engineer, was born just outside the area at Stockport, but spent his last fifteen years inside it at Stancliffe Hall, Darley Dale. The house is now a preparatory school, but his name is trebly commemorated in the village by the Whitworth Memorial Institute, Baths and Hospital, erected after his death by the trustees of his estate at a cost of £105,000, and in the park behind the Institute is a gaunt memorial to Sir Joseph and his second wife. The mile-long New Road through the village, as straight as a Whitworth rifle, was his work, though intended less as a gift to the village than as a means of bypassing two level crossings that hindered his passage to the station.

Sebastian de Ferranti (1864–1930) left less visible trace of his twenty-four years' residence in the Peak—at Grindleford and then Baslow, both within commuting distance of his works at Hollinwood, near Oldham—except at Baslow Hall, where his passion for electricity was not confined to working hours. He was a 'do-it-yourself' man, who attempted to heat his house by using a heavy oil-engine to supply power to ingenious ceiling-radiators. But power failures were frequent and his family spent many long winter evenings huddled in fur coats. When the system was abandoned, electric fires were installed in every conceivable place and even in places that were quite inconceivable. The house became an electrician's paradise, with an electric laundry, electric lawnmower, a tennis court lit by electricity, and every labour-saving device that could be operated electrically, in addition to an early attempt at battery poultry farming that ended with the electrocution of a number of chickens.

If the Peak has produced few great men, it has reared two great women: Bess of Hardwick and Florence Nightingale. To be completely scrupulous, neither was born in the Peak, but both belonged so much to it that the fact may be ignored.

Elizabeth Hardwick was born in 1520 at Hardwick in the Old Hall, whose ruins stand alongside the magnificent Elizabethan house she built herself in the 1590s. Her story is so remarkable that it deserves a whole volume rather than the single paragraph that must serve here. Having married first at the age of twelve a young neighbouring landowner named Robert Barlow, and became a widow within months, she went on to three further marriages in ascending order of wealth and status. Her last three husbands, Sir William Cavendish, Sir William St Lo and the Earl of Shrewsbury were all widowers whom Bess persuaded, before accepting their proposals, to will their possessions to her. This 'intolerable but irresistible' woman, as A. L. Rowse described her, 'lived', in the words of an earlier historian, 'to a great age continually flattered but seldom deceived, and died immensely rich and without a friend'. Her income then was said to be £60,000 a year, and Horace Walpole claimed in 1760 that her estates at that time brought in £200,000 a year. Many of these estates lay in the Peak, with Chatsworth at their heart. Chatsworth was the first of the many houses she built and it was there that she enjoyed her happiest marriage, bore her six children and founded the Cavendish dynasty whose power and influence in and around the Peak has continued ever since.

Bess used her immense drive, organising ability and zest for life in the interests of herself and her families. Three centuries later, Florence Nightingale, who shared at least the first two qualities, used them in the interests of others. Though she was born in the city from which she derived her name, Florence was very much a child of the Peak. Lea Hurst, built by her parents and later decried by her mother because it 'only had fifteen bedrooms', was her first English home. It was from there that she gained her first experience of social work in the nearby village of Holloway and 'met the evils of nineteenth-century industrialism—drunkenness, overcrowding and brutality', and it was to Lea Hurst—today a home for the elderly—that she returned from the Crimea, walking alone up the hill from Whatstandwell Station to avoid the crowds who waited to acclaim her elsewhere.

There is a case for ending this book at that point; with this solitary, middle-aged lady trudging up the hill alone, so anxious to avoid any display of emotion. It somehow sums up the character of Peakland people, as do those other qualities of energy, determination and moral courage that she displayed, qualities which Defoe, Hudson and others failed to notice. But Florence's greatest exploits were performed far away from the Peak. So it is to a lesser-known figure that I must turn to end this book.

The name of Fred Heardman will mean little to people outside the Peak, for it has appeared only rarely in print. Before he died a year or two ago, Fred kept the Nag's Head Inn at Edale for many years and made an excellent job of it. But he was much more than just a highly successful innkeeper. On three sides of his inn the ground rose steeply to one of England's last surviving wildernesses. Within a mile or two of his inn it was possible for people to lose themselves and die of exposure. Some did so; others would have done if it had not been for Fred and his customers and friends who eventually developed into the Edale Mountain Rescue Team, now part of the highly organised Peak District Mountain Rescue Organisation, which has come to stand for ramblers, pot-holers and climbers in the Peak as the lifeboat service does for sailors.

When Britain's first full-time National Park Warden— Tom Tomlinson—was appointed in the Peak in 1954 his first headquarters was, naturally enough, Fred Heardman's Nag's Head Inn at Edale, and at the same time Fred, to quote from the Peak Park Board's Report for 1974, 'hit upon the idea of letting the visitors to his country pub share his secrets of the wild hills and the valleys around them'. The Report goes on: 'With maps, books, charts, with flint microliths and other treasures he has found on the moors, but most of all with his unique personality and enthusiasm, he created a place which became a "must" for those who sought to enjoy and understand the meaning of the countryside.' Almost accidentally, Fred Heardman sowed the seed for what is now a highly efficient information service in the Peak Park. The first full-time information officer was appointed nine years later, but in a sense, Fred was the Peak's first information officer, just as he was in the same sense its first unofficial warden and rescue service organiser. He also thought out some of the now famous walks across the Peak, such as the 'Three Inns', from the Isle of Skye above Holmfirth, via the Snake Inn to the Cat and Fiddle.

'To me', an ex-Warden told me, 'Fred Heardman personified the Peak.' Fred loved the Peak in the same way that a sailor loves the sea; knowing its signs, understanding its moods, appreciating that love first demands respect. To Fred, as to Dr Russell, the Peak was 'a sort of Paradise'—though as a man of the Peak, he might not have put it like that—but he knew that even in Paradise the stranger has to tread warily.

BIBLIOGRAPHY

Byng, J. (ed Andrews). *The Torrington Diaries 1781–94* (1954)
Christian, Roy. *Old English Customs* (1966)
Clapham, A. R. (ed). *Flora of Derbyshire* (1969)
Coleman, Terry. *The Railway Navvies* (1965)
Defoe, D. *A Tour Through England and Wales* (1724)
Derby Museum. *Natural History of Derbyshire* (ND)
Dodd, A. E. and E. M. *Peakland Roads and Trackways* (1974)
Edwards, K. C. *The Peak District* (1972)
English Life Publications. *Derbyshire Guide* (1974)
Fiennes, C. (ed Morris). *Journeys of Celia Fiennes* (1947)
Firth, J. B. *Highways and Byways of Derbyshire* (1905)
Ford, T. D. and Rieuwarts, J. M. *Lead Mining in the Peak District* (1968)
Harris, H. *Industrial Archaeology of the Peak District* (1971)
HMSO (ed Monkhouse). *Peak District National Park* (1960)
Kirkham, Nellie. *Derbyshire Lead Mining Through the Centuries* (1968)
Monkhouse, Patrick. *On Foot in the Peak* (1932)
Nicholson, C. P., Barnes, P. *Railways in the Peak District* (1971)
Nixon, Frank. *The Industrial Archaeology of Derbyshire* (1969)
Palmer, William T. *The River Mersey* (1944)
Pearsall, W. H. *Mountains and Moorlands* (1950)
Pevsner, Sir N. *Derbyshire* (1953)
Porteous, Crichton. *Portrait of the Peak* (1963)
Redfern, Roger A. *Portrait of the Pennines* (1969)
Spencer, B. and Robey, J. *The Derbyshire Wye and Lathkill Dale* (1973)
Tarn, J. N. *The Peak District National Park—Its Architecture* (1972)
Unsworth, Walt. *Portrait of the River Derwent* (1971)

PERIODICALS

Derbyshire Life and Countryside (formerly *Derbyshire Countryside*)
Derbyshire Archaeological Journal
Derbyshire Miscellany
Derbyshire Naturalists' Trust Newsletters
Peak Park News
Peak Park Planning Board, Annual Reports
Railway Magazine

INDEX

INDEX

INDEX